ROUTES

IN

SIKKIM

COMPILED IN THE

INTELLIGENCE BRANCH OF THE QUARTERMASTER GENERAL'S DEPARTMENT IN INDIA.

BY

CAPTAIN W. F. O'CONNOR,
ROYAL GARRISON ARTILLERY.

CALCUTTA:

OFFICE OF THE SUPERINTENDENT OF GOVERNMENT PRINTING, INDIA.

1900.

AUTHORITIES CONSULTED.

1. Routes in Sikkim, 1894.

2. Report on the Chumbi Valley by Captain F. C. Colomb, 42nd Gurkha Rifles, 1896.

3. Report on Roads from Tangu and Lachung by Surgeon-Captain A. Pearse, A.M.S., 1895.

4. Report on Road from Gantok to Giaogong by Brigadier-General Yeatman-Biggs, C.B., 1896.

5. Report on Road from Giaogong to Momay Samdong by Brigadier-General Yeatman-Biggs, C.B., 1896.

6. Reports on Roads in Lho-Nak by Lieutenant W. F. O'Connor, R. A., 1896.

7. Hooker's Himalayan Journals.

8. Reports of Great Trigonometrical Survey.

9. Notes on Roads in Sikkim by Political Officer, Sikkim, 1897, 1899, and 1900.

10. Routes in Asia.

11. Account of an embassy to the Court of Teshoo Lama in Tibet, etc., by Captain Turner, 1783.

12. Notes on Roads near Talung by Lieutenant W. Strong, R. A., 1897.

I. B. Diary No. $\frac{4 \text{ of } 1898}{\text{Sikkim}}$.

SIKKIM ROUTES.

No.	From	To	Remarks.	Page.
1	Jalpaiguri	Padong	......	3
2	Siliguri	Teesta Bridge	......	5
3	Darjeeling	Gnathong	*Viâ* Rhenock	7
4	Do.	Gantok	Ditto	12
5	Do.	Do.	*Viâ* Rungpo	15
6	Do.	Do.	*Viâ* Namchi	16
7	Do.	Do.	*Viâ* Sedam	19
8	Do.	Pamionchi	*Viâ* Singla Bazar	20
9	Do.	Chiabhanjan	*Viâ* Nepal frontier road	22
10	Do.	Do.	*Viâ* Gokh	25
11	Do.	Samatek	*Viâ* Namchi and Teesta valley	26
12	Gnathong	Chumbi	*Viâ* Jelep La	27
13	Do.	Do.	*Viâ* Nathu La	31
14	Do.	Gantok	*Viâ* Lagyap La	33
15	Do.	Cho La	......	35
16	Do.	Donchuk La and Doka La	......	38
17	Do.	Yak La	......	40
18	Donchukthang	Jelep La	......	42
19	Yak La	Rabdo Tso	......	ib.
20	Gantok	Cho La	......	43
21	Do.	Yak La	......	44
22	Do.	Giaogong	......	45
23	Do.	Donkhya La	......	51
23(a)	Momay Samdong	Karpo La	......	55
24	Do.	Pamionchi	*Viâ* Song	56
25	Do.	Naku La	*Viâ* Talung	57
26	Lachung	Thanka La	......	ib.
26(a)	Chumbocum Gorge	Pato La	......	58
27	Lachung	Lamteng	*Viâ* Beurm La	59
28	Do.	Ghora La	......	61
28(a)	Tukpoo Como	Sethang	*Viâ* Cheychima	63
29	Lachung	Momay Samdong	Ditto	ib.
30	Giaogong	Donkhya La	*Viâ* Cholamo lakes	64
31	Do.	Momay Samdong	*Viâ* Sebu La	ib.
32	Tangu	Sitong	*Viâ* Longtong La and Pallung La	65
33	Do.	Sebu La	......	66
34	Do.	Naku La	*Viâ* Lungna La	67
35	Tebli	Choten Nima La	......	68
36	Zemu Samdong	Naku La	*Viâ* Zemu Chu	70

Route No. 1.

FROM JALPAIGURI TO PADONG (ON THE DARJEELING-GNATHONG ROAD).

Authorities and date.—MAJOR A. A. A. KINLOCH, 1877, AND CAPTAIN O. B. ZOUCH-DARRAH, THE QUEEN'S REGIMENT, 1893.

No. of stages.	Names of stages.	DISTANCES IN MILES.		REMARKS.
		Inter-mediate.	Total.	
				General direction, north.
1	KIRINTI THANA	12	12	Road raised and quite flat between Jalpaiguri and the Teesta river, which is reached at 5 miles; no villages are passed, and there is no drinking water along this portion of the road. The bed of the Teesta is a mile wide, and the stream is broken up into many channels, which are constantly changing; it is crossed by a ferry consisting of rafts constructed of two country boats, each 35 × 9 feet, lashed together, a rough platform 20 feet square forming the deck. Each ferry raft is capable of crossing four native carts with their bullocks (unharnessed) per trip, or six laden mules or three field guns; there are in all eight ferry boats. The Teesta is quite unfordable,* and its water is muddy.
				Road now rises imperceptibly for 6 miles, being raised 10 feet, and passing through cultivated country up to camp. At Kirinti Thana there is a post and telegraph office and a police out-post; no supplies procurable. Water from the Chel river. On left of road, close to the river bank, is a good camping ground large enough for two battalions. From Kirinti an unmetalled road leads left (west) to Changmari Hât, a small *bazar* 3 miles distant, where markets are held on Mondays and Wednesdays.
2	CHEL RIVER	10	22	At 4¼ miles a broad unmetalled cart track on an embankment leads right to Bataigol railway station. At 6 miles pass Adhadanga, a village of some 30 huts, and one mile on enter forest reserve; road embanked and ditched. Cross the Chel river, a fordable stream with a gravel and sand bottom with a rapid current one to two and a half feet deep, flowing in a channel 150 yards wide. Space to north of river sufficient to camp one battalion; good water from river. A larger force could camp in the neighbouring rice fields, but the crops are not off the ground till the end of the year. Nearest *bazar*, whence supplies are procurable, is Dam Dim, 4½ miles north.
3	SOMBARIA HAT	14¼	36¼	For first mile through forest and rice fields, then enter tea gardens, crossing at 1 mile a stream spanned by a bridge constructed of iron rails and stout logs; roadway 15 feet. At 2 miles cross a second similar bridge over a sluggish stream 3 feet deep. At 4½ miles reach Dam Dim, the largest bazar north of Jalpaiguri in this part of the district. The village consists of some 40 thatched wooden houses and 20 wooden houses roofed with corrugated iron. Post and telegraph offices; supplies available in large quantities; water bad from wells. Dam Dim is the terminus of the new railway from Jalpaiguri *viâ* Bataigol, which was opened about the end of 1893. Thence through tea gardens, the road being unmetalled from the 7th mile onward and following the left bank of the Chel river. Sombaria Hât is a *bazar* of some 35 substantial wooden huts with thatched roofs; supplies available after due notice. The camping ground lies immediately to the north of the *bazar*, and is sufficient for half a battalion; water from the Chel river. To the east of the road lies the Gornbatham plateau, where two brigades would find room to encamp.
				A good cart track leads from Sombaria Hât to Siliguri, distant 28 miles, *viâ* the Manabari Tea Estate.
				Elevation of Sombaria Hât, 1,000 feet.

* It is possible, here and there, to ford the Teesta on elephants during the winter months.   W. F. O'C.

Route No. 1—*contd.*

No. of stages.	Names of stages.	Distances.		Remarks.
		Inter- mediate.	Total.	
4	LABAH . . .	13¾	50	Road now enters the hills and becomes a six-foot track, generally cut in the hill-side; it is unmetalled, but is firm and in good repair. The whole of this stage is through forest, and the road is well shaded. For first mile road level with rice fields on either side, a stream being crossed at ⅓ mile, at which point a road branches off left up the Nimlo hill to Pagoo tea estate, crossing the Chel* river by small bamboo bridge. Between 1 mile and 1½ miles many small unbridged streams cross the road, flowing from a high ridge to right of road; at 1½ miles cross a large mountain stream by two bridges spanning two arms separated by an island. Each bridge is 20 feet long and 6 feet above low water level; they are constructed of bamboo, and have a 6-foot roadway passable to transport animals, but not to wheeled traffic. At 2 miles heavy bamboo jungle and high cliffs to the right of the road. At 2¼ miles the Chel river is within 100 yards off, and 100 feet below the road to the left; enter a narrow defile between the Daling Ma ridge and the Chel river, and at 3 miles ascend at a slope of 5° through dense jungle; road here in bad repair; a little further on the road passes through tea plantations and is not so steep, but continues steadily ascending. Cross a small stream roughly bridged at 4¾ miles, bridge of bamboo 20 feet long and too light for baggage animals, which can ford river immediately below bridge; to right of road are high forest-clad hills, while to the left are fields and a few thatched huts; road here in bad repair. Ambiokh is reached at 5½ miles; village consists of a few huts and two Hindu temples; no supplies procurable; good water and fuel in abundance, and a camping ground sufficient for 3 brigades. Half a mile to the east of, and above Ambiokh, is Daling Kot or Fort Daling (elevation 3,550 feet), now in ruins and overgrown with dense jungle; a steep, narrow path circling round the hill forms the only approach to the fort.
				At 6 miles the Chel river is crossed by a strong log bridge 57 feet in span and 23 feet above the stream level in the cold season. Strong stone piers support the bridge on either bank, and the roadway is 6 feet wide in the clear. The Chel river is here a torrent, 20 yards wide, flowing in a bed much obstructed by boulders, with a depth of from 3 to 6 feet; the gorge of the river is 100 yards wide. Hence road ascends by sharp zigzags, and is then level for half a mile, crossing several small mountain streams which are spanned by bridges sufficiently strong to bear pack animals. At 7 miles the village of Keithongshin, consisting of five or six thatched huts, is reached. The stage may be broken here if necessary, as there is an open space on either side of the road sufficient for two battalions to encamp, and an abundant and good water-supply is available within 100 yards of the camp; camp is well sheltered and fuel is plentiful, but no supplies are available. In the next half mile road crosses five small bridged mountain streams. At 7¾ miles the road is less level, and for the next half mile there is a steep ascent at a gradient of from 20° to 25°, after which ascent is easier up to the 11th mile; gradients about 8°. Country, thin forest with an undergrowth of bracken and scrub; pass the Pashiteng forest hut at 11 miles; here there is a camping ground for a couple of companies, and hence road is fairly level for one mile, after which there is a sharp descent to a stream at 12¼ miles; at 12 miles a track on left leads to the Pagoo tea estate on the southern slopes of Nimlo hill, distant 10 miles. Ascend from stream for ½ a mile at a slope of 8°; road cut in hillside, then descend and finally ascend to camp half a mile short of which a bridle path on left leads to Tolleia Basti and another right, fit for pedestrians only, to the Bhutan frontier *viâ* Pankasari (3 miles distant) at Richi La, and continues along the ridge defining the Bhutan-Sikkim frontier to Shalambi, about 1½ miles south-west of Gnathong.

* Or Chi Chu.

No. of stages.	Names of stages.	DISTANCES.		REMARKS.
		Inter-mediate	Total.	
				Labah is a village of 15 to 20 thatched huts, inhabited by Nepalese, at an elevation of 6,600 feet. There is a good dry camping ground to the left of the road sufficient for one battalion. Water from a spring 300 yards from camp; no supplies available.
5	PADONG	12	62	Road in good repair throughout this stage. Ascend gradually for 1¾ miles; at 2 miles descend at a slope of about 10°. Here a good bridle path leads right down a long spur to the Jesuit Mission Chapel, 6 miles distant, opposite Padong, and thence to Rhenock. Road now through bamboo jungle, descending at first steeply and then more gently. At 3½ miles pass an open space in the forest called Mirig Naugi; here half a battalion could encamp; nearest water-supply half a mile down the hill-side. At 4¼ miles a path leads off left downhill to a stream of good water 400 yards distant. Descend gradually along summit of ridge and descend steeply by a zigzag for 200 yards; track narrow. At 7 miles pass the Rissum Bungalow at an elevation of 6,410 feet; here a company could encamp, and a battalion, were the ground on the southern hill slope cleared; water obtainable half a mile down hill-side; the bungalow, which is situated on the summit of a hill, from which a fine view is obtained, is approached from the road by a zigzag path; road now fairly level for a short distance, when a good path branches off left to Tolleia Basti, distant 10 miles; here main road descends steeply for a quarter of a mile by a steep zigzag. At 8 miles the track bifurcates, one branch striking off left to Kalimpong joining Route No. 3, about 1¾ miles on. Road now level through dense wood; cross a stream of good water and about 500 yards on pass Chumeikchin monastery at 10¼ miles; here the main road from Darjeeling to Gnathong is struck, and is traversed for 1¾ miles to Padong (*vide* Route No. 3).

Route No. 2.

SILIGURI to the TEESTA SUSPENSION BRIDGE (on the Darjeeling-Gnathong road).

Authorities.—QUARTER MASTER GENERAL'S DEPARTMENTAL MEMORANDUM DATED 1ST DECEMBER 1887, LIEUTENANT C. VICKERS, THE QUEEN'S REGIMENT, 1894, AND LIEUTENANT W. F. O'CONNOR, R.A., 1897.

No. of stages.	Names of stages.	DISTANCES.		REMARKS.
		Inter-mediate.	Total.	
				General direction, north.
				The road generally follows the Teesta valley and passes through a district in which malaria is very prevalent during the rainy season. It is passable to carts throughout and is well shaded: the angles, however, are sharp; and as the road in the hills is narrow and there are no parapet walls, cart traffic by night is attended with danger.
1	SEVOKE	11½	11½	Road leaves the Siliguri railway station and runs northwest for half a mile: it then turns due north and passes through rice fields along an embankment for

c

No. of stages.	Names of stages.	DISTANCES.		REMARKS.
		Inter-mediate.	Total.	
				5½ miles, when the Terai is entered, through which road runs in a direct line for the remainder of the stage. At 7¼ miles cross a stream by a strong wooden bridge 34 feet long in 3 spans, and at 7½ miles a second bridge of the same type 14 feet long. Pass a small village at 5 miles. The Terai forest becomes more dense as Sevoke is approached. Sevoke is a small clearing in the Terai with a few bamboo shanties, and a *bazar* consisting of about a dozen houses inhabited mostly by Nepalese settlers; a few maunds of rice or *bhuta* could generally be procured here. There is a shed for sheltering baggage animals, 40 feet by 18 feet. The village is situated near the junction of the Sevoke stream, a *nala* containing a few inches of water, with the Teesta river. Water from the Teesta, which flows within 500 yards of camp; ground available for a brigade. Sevoke is unhealthy at most times of the year owing to its situation at the immediate foot of the hills, but during the months of December and January it is quite healthy and the climate pleasant. Bamboo fodder plentiful. Road, 12 to 14 feet wide, in good repair and metalled. Passable to carts. There is a ferry here across the Teesta connecting Sevoke with the tea-gardens of the Doars; there are 2 boats, each about 18 feet long, hollowed out of logs of wood, which can take about 10 persons at a time.
2	RIANG	13½	25	Road now enters the hills and runs up the right bank of the Teesta, being cut out of the steep hillside from 10 to 50 feet above the level of the stream: the width of the metalled portion is now from 7 to 8 feet, and the total width from 10 to 12 feet; the road is level and in good repair, metal and bridging timber being ready to hand. Along this stage the road is liable to be blocked by boulders slipping from the hill-slopes above. At 5 miles cross the Kali-Jora stream, which is crossed by an iron bridge 120 feet long and 8 feet wide in the clear; bridge consists of a single span resting on stone abutments, 13 feet above the cold weather level of the stream. At Kali-Jora there is a dâk bungalow and a small *bazar*. At 12½ miles cross the Riang river by an iron suspension bridge 135 feet long and 7 feet broad in the clear.* Numerous other strong wooden bridges and culverts are crossed. Riang is a small *bazar* consisting of about a dozen houses and a Police Thana at the junction of the Riang river with the Teesta. Camping ground to the left of the road, to the north of and behind the village. Dâk bungalow; country thick jungle throughout. A small quantity of rice and *bhuta* can generally be obtained here; bamboo fodder plentiful. A road branches off here to the left, leading up to Poomong and other tea estates, and joining the Ghoom-Pashok road at the 8th mile, at a distance of about 10 miles from Riang (*vide* Route No. 3); elevation of Riang 625 feet.
3	TEESTA BRIDGE	4½	29½	Road good and level throughout. Numerous strong wooden culverts are crossed, and at 2 miles and 4 miles two streams are crossed by well-built wooden bridges 60 and 54 feet long respectively. At the bridge there is a P. W. D. bungalow, elevation 710 feet, a post office, and a small *bazar*. No camping ground, and water-supply scanty from a rivulet flowing through the *bazar* about 300 yards from the bridge. Teesta water generally very muddy. Small quantities of rice and *bhuta* could generally be obtained; bamboo fodder plentiful in the jungles. Troops would not ordinarily halt here, but would move on, if making for Gantok, to Kalimpong; 10 miles further on by cart-road, or 7 by bridle-path (*vide* Route No. 3). Road along the right bank of Teesta from bridge leading to Darjeeling either *via* Pashok or Rangit (*vide* Route No. 3). Elevation of Teesta bridge 710 feet.

* The floods of 1899 did a great deal of damage at the Riang river; hundreds of yards of the roadway were destroyed, and the bridge had to be dismantled. At the time of writing (Aug. 1900) the road is only passable for coolies and unladen animals.

Route No. 3.

From DARJEELING to GNATHONG (*viâ* Kalimpong, Rhenock, and Lingtu).

Authority and date.—Sikkim Routes, 1894, and Captain F. C. Colomb 42nd Gurkha Rifles, May 1895.

No. of stages.	Names of stages.	Distances in Miles.		Remarks.
		Intermediate.	Total.	
1	Pashok . . .	17½	17½	From Darjeeling a good almost level bridle-path leads round the eastern face of the hill to Jor Bungalow, 3 miles.

From Darjeeling a good almost level bridle-path leads round the eastern face of the hill to Jor Bungalow, 3 miles.

Jor Bungalow is a considerable *bazar* on the saddle between the Jalapahar and Senchal peaks; it is close to the Ghoom railway station.

Troops arriving from the plains would start from Jor Bungalow, thus diminishing the march to Pashok by 3 miles.

There is no recognised camping-ground at Jor Bungalow, but small bodies of men could encamp on the Jalapahar hill above the Ghoom railway station, and also on the mountain battery parade ground.

The Pashok road turns off left from the southern end of the bazar, elevation 7,370 feet, and is a level cart-road for 3 miles; at its narrowest it is 12 feet broad and runs through forest, there being several open spaces suitable for shunting places. At 5½ miles (2½ from Jor Bungalow) road left to Rungaroon Dâk and forest bungalows, situated about 1,000 feet down the hill-side. At the 6th mile (3rd from Jor Bungalow) is a small village and wood-cutters' settlement, and here 3 roads turn off to the right: one up Senchal hill practicable for ponies or mountain batteries; the centre one to a new forest bungalow 3 or 4 miles distant, and the third to the Government chinchona plantations; here there is camping space for two companies if scattered. Hence for 3 miles the road has been realigned as a cart road, the new trace running along the southern face of the spur. This new portion is a good 12 feet metalled road almost level. The old road, which runs along the northern face of the hill, joins it again at the 9th mile (6th from Jor Bungalow). At 9½ miles (6½ from Jor Bungalow) the road forks, the lower or left-hand branch being the old road, which has been allowed to fall into disrepair. At 11 miles (8 from Jor Bungalow) road right to Poomong and other tea plantations, which eventually debouches on to the Teesta valley road at Riang, a distance of about 10 miles. A well kept road, too steep for carts, but excellent for mules or horses. At 2 miles along this road reach Hoom forest bungalow, where 2 companies, or a section of a mountain battery, could be camped. Water from streams crossing the road, bamboo fodder.

At 13 miles, where the road under report emerges from the dense forest through which it has hitherto passed, there is a forest bungalow and an open space on which ½ regiment could encamp; water, fuel and fodder plentiful. Name of this place is Lopchu. A path turns off to the left to the Lopchu tea estate. The last mile down to Lopchu is very steep. Road hence is a strong bridle-path averaging 6 feet in width, and the country is alternate scrub jungle and cultivation; a few small stone bridges spanning unimportant streams are crossed.

At the 14th mile enter tea garden, and the road descends steeply, till at the 16th mile the tea factory of the Pashok tea estate is passed; here there is always a plentiful water-supply. Road steep to 17th mile where enter forest; and at 17½ reach Pashok bungalow.

The bungalow is built in a clearing in sâl forest above and to the north of the road; accommodation 4 rooms, no servants kept, except a care-taker; in the immediate

Route No. 3—*contd.*

No. of stages.	Names of stages.	DISTANCES.		REMARKS.
		Inter-mediate.	Total.	
				vicinity of the bungalow there is space for ½ a battalion to encamp, if scattered, on fairly level ground. Water: there are 2 small pools about 1,000 yards from the bungalow in a northerly direction on the northern face of the hill; a narrow path leads to one; and to reach the other, it is necessary to scramble down the hill-side, beyond where the path ceases, through tea bushes. Transport animals may be watered at the 13th mile (from Jor Bungalow) by the Pashok tea estate factory, where there are 3 or 4 large barrels on the road always kept filled by an excellent stream of water. Grass and bamboo fodder obtainable in plenty two miles down the hill-side to the south. Fuel plentiful; no supplies.
				The road on the whole is good, and is practicable for animal carriage, infantry and mountain artillery. There are no gradients greater than 1 in 8, and no bridges or streams of any importance.
				Elevation of bungalow, 3,300 feet.
2	KALIMPONG . . .	13½	31	Descend steadily for 2½ miles to the Teesta valley, elevation about 700 feet; road, a good bridle-path through sāl and other forest throughout; average gradient ⅛, width of road 12 feet, but in places it narrows to 8 feet. At 2½ miles the cart-road, which connects Siliguri with Badamtam *viâ* the valleys of the Teesta and Rangit is reached; from this spot it is, by the cart-road, 30 miles to Siliguri and 18 to Darjeeling. The cart-road is now followed for ⅛ mile to the Teesta bridge; it is 8 feet wide at its narrowest, and lies along the bank of the river some 30 feet above its flood-level. Quarter of a mile above, where the bridle-path joins the cart-road, the Pashok Khola is crossed by a good wooden bridge 20 yards long and passable to carts; stream would form no obstacle except in the rains. Two villages are passed, the second of which, Teesta Pul, is at the bridge itself; here there is a post office, P.W.D. bungalow, and an agency of the British-Bhutan Carrying Company. At Teesta Pul four or five carts may generally be hired without notice, but no coolies are available. The Teesta flows through a narrow, rocky, wooded valley; is nowhere fordable, and is from 50 to 100 yards wide according to the season of the year. The river is spanned by a wire rope suspension bridge 100 yards long and 8 feet wide in the clear, and about 100 feet above high-water level, elevation 710 feet; it is passable to infantry and mountain guns singly. Carts also can cross the bridge.
				From the bridge to Kalimpong is a climb of 3,300 feet either by a fair cart-road in 10 miles or by a bridle-path in about 7. The first two miles are through the forest, and a small village is then reached where a good stream of water crosses the road, and where there is camping-ground for one regiment in forest. At ½ mile above Teesta bridge the new Teesta valley road branches off (*vide* Route No. 5).
				Road then emerges on a gently sloping, closely cultivated hill-side, dotted with villages and small settlements. The last two miles the road is almost level and 15 feet wide, winding round a well cultivated valley. Average gradient of the bridle-path $\frac{1}{10}$; the cart-road is not metalled and becomes very heavy after rain; carts plying up the hill should only carry the lightest loads. One small wooden bridge, 33 feet long and 6 feet 6 inches wide, is crossed, but the stream which it spans forms no obstacle. The bridle-path and cart-road unite 2 miles short of Kalimpong. The bridle-path, although steep, can be used for infantry or mountain artillery.
				The dâk bungalow, which has four large rooms, is situated in a clearing in the forest to the west of and above Kalimpong Bazar, and is reached

Route No. 3—*contd.*

No. of stages.	Names of stages.	DISTANCES.		REMARKS.
		Inter-mediate.	Total.	
				by a path which turns off right about ½ mile short of the *bazar*. A force of 500 men could encamp on the flat grassy compound of the bungalow if crowded together. Water good, from a pipe in the compound, the supply being about two gallons per minute. Fuel in plenty in immediate vicinity. Fodder can only be cut on a pass from the Tenduk Raja whose agent at Kalimpong can supply any quantity on notice being given. Bamboos plentiful about hill-side.
				Kalimpong is a large *bazar*, elevation 4,000 feet, on a flat saddle, from which the slope on either side is gentle and highly cultivated. The houses are of wood with corrugated-iron roofs. There are a large number of bunniahs' shops through which supplies in considerable quantities could be obtained on 10 days' notice being given. Post and telegraph offices, church and head-quarters of Scotch Missionary Society. To the east of the *bazar* is a fairly level camping-ground large enough for two regiments; good and abundant water from a stream close at hand; good grazing for animals on neighbouring hill-slopes.
				A path leads from the *bazar* to the new Teesta valley road, joining it at Mali Ghat, 3 miles from Teesta bridge (see Route No. 5). Half a mile beyond the *bazar* another path leads across the ridge to the left and hence down to the new Teesta valley road, joining it at the 9th mile from Teesta bridge (see Route No. 5.)
	TEESTA BRIDGE	18½	18¼	*Alternative Route.** [The Teesta bridge can also be reached from Darjeeling by the Rangit river road, which leaves the "chaurasta" at Darjeeling and zigzags down the Lebong spur, reaching its foot at an elevation of 1,000 feet in 10 miles. Hence the road is almost level following the right bank of the Rangit river. It has no gradients of more than ₁₂ and is passable for carts throughout. There are several small timber bridges, the largest of which is at the 14th mile (about 50 feet span). The junction of the Great Rangit and Teesta rivers is at the 17th mile, where there is a level piece of ground which would give camping space for over 1,000 men, but the jungle would have to be cleared. This road meets the Jor Bungalow-Kalimpong road, ⅛ mile short of the Teesta bridge. (For the first half of this road, see Route No. 6.)]
	PADONG	12	43	From Kalimpong to Padong is 12 miles, but if the march is commenced from the dâk bungalow it is increased by ¼ a mile.
				The road throughout is a broad bridle-path, along the first 5 or 6 miles of which carts travel. Average width 12 feet; no streams of any importance crossed. For 9 miles from Kalimpong the road ascends steadily, gradients not greater than ₁₆; the first 8 miles are through cultivation, many small villages being passed, and the road passing over the eastern slopes of a range, the highest peaks of which rise some 1,500 feet above the road. At the 9th mile forest is entered and a small village called Poyun Argarah is reached; here the road from Jalpaiguri *via* Rissum, Labah and Daling (*vide* Route No. 1) joins in. At 9½ miles road reaches its highest point 5,400 feet and crosses a saddle in thick tree jungle. The descent is apparently too steep for carts, though carts carrying 5 or 6 maunds occasionally ply between Kalimpong and Padong. On nearing the end of stage the road emerges from the forest, and the hill slopes below the road are gently sloping and closely cultivated. There is water along the road for the first 2 or 3 miles, after which there are no streams until after the saddle is crossed.
				The Padong bungalow is situated on an open grassy hill-side at an elevation of 4,760 feet and contains four rooms; immediately to the south of the bungalow is

The cart road along the right bank of the Rangit from the foot of the Badamtam spur to the junction of the Rangit with the Teesta was entirely destroyed by the flood in 1899. At the time of writing (Aug. 1900) a track has been made passable for animals.

Route No. 3—*contd.*

No. of stages.	Names of stages.	Distances in Miles.		Remarks.
		Inter-mediate.	Total.	
				a grassy, fairly level camping-ground sufficient to accommodate two regiments. Water (from a spring to the north of and just below the bungalow) scanty, except during the rains. Transport animals can be watered from this same stream about 200 yards below the road, where the stream expands in some marshy bottoms. There is a certain amount of grazing for animals about the hill-sides, and a little bamboo is available, otherwise fodder is not very plentiful. Fuel in plenty from woods above the bungalow.
				Padong village is ½ a mile beyond and below the bungalow; it consists of a collection of wooden houses (2 or 3 of which are of considerable size and could be utilized as barracks or hospitals), post office and a stone church. For the first 9 miles it would require 500 pioneers 3 days to put the road in good order for carts, but beyond this the road is too steep and requires to be realigned. This would take the same number of men 10 days or a fortnight.
				A branch road to Gantok leaves Padong left.
4	Ari	8	51	A steep zigzag descent for 4 miles to the Rishi Chu, elevation 2,030 feet; road, a wide bridle-path, in fair order, and paved with cobble stones in places, through cultivation, except in the valley bottom where the jungle is fairly thick. Average gradient 1 in 6.
				No water along the road until the Rishi is reached. The stream is a considerable mountain torrent which is unfordable in the rains; it is crossed by a strong timber lattice bridge of two spans, 17 and 21 yards long, with a 7½ feet clear roadway about 30 feet above the cold weather level of the river. The ruins of the old bridge, which could be repaired without much difficulty, are 50 yards up stream.
				Hence an equally steep ascent for 4 miles to Ari; the first mile up from the river is through tree forest, the road being narrow and rough and paved with cobble stones. More open country is then entered and at 1½ miles Rhenock Bazar is reached. The *bazar*, elevation 3,030 feet, consists of a single street with a small collection of wooden houses, thatched with grass, on either side. Two fair-sized houses useful as barracks; good water supply on the spot and fuel obtainable. Post and telegraph office and two-roomed dâk bungalow. Country in vicinity open and fairly well cultivated.
				The principal man of the place is a Nepali named Chander Bhir, who owns a considerable property in the neighbourhood, and would make arrangements for coolies, supplies, etc.
				From Rhenock Bazar road left to Gantok distant two marches (*vide* Route No. 4).
				Hence the road is good, paved in places, passing through cultivation and patches of jungle, to Ari. Water at intervals along road above Rhenock Bazar. Average gradient of ascent 1 in 10.
				The Ari bungalow is situated on a fairly level spur at an elevation of 4,500 feet and 200 feet below the saddle where the road crosses the Rhenock ridge. The bungalow is a small rest-house with 3 rooms. Half a regiment could camp on the spur, but the grass swarms with leeches; fuel plentiful; water scarce from a conduit on roadside just above the rest-house. No village or supplies. No post office. Fodder must be arranged for from Rhenock Bazar.
5	Sedongchen . .	13	64	Ascend 200 feet and cross the Rhenock ridge and descend 4 miles to the Rongli Chu by a very rough bridle-path paved in places passing through tree jungle throughout.

Route No. 3—*contd.*

No. of stages.	Names of stages.	Distances. Inter-mediate.	Total.	Remarks.
				Average gradients 1 in 8 ; road 8 feet wide. Half a mile short of the Rongli a stream is crossed by a rough log bridge, 12 yards long ; roadway 5 feet, no hand rails. Stream fordable at any time, but banks steep ; they are however easily ramped, as the soil is soft. Hence it is half a mile by a level road to the Rongli Chu, on the left bank of which stands Rongli village, a miserable collection of some dozen grass huts. No supplies.
				There is drinking water along the road throughout the descent. Elevation of Rongli 2,590 feet ; no bungalow now exists here. The Rongli Chu is only fordable in the cold weather when it is at its lowest ; it is crossed by a new iron truss bridge of one span, 30 yards long, supported on strong stone abutments ; road-way 5 feet wide in the clear and 50 feet above the cold weather level of the stream.
				The old road *viâ* Lingtam turns to the left and ascends the hill-side immediately after crossing the bridge, but is no longer kept up. The new road turns to the right and follows the right bank of the Rongli Chu occasion-ally rising to circumvent precipitous banks. It is through dense forest and is infested by myriads of leeches, and is in places not more than 5 feet wide, though the average is about 8 feet. At the 7th mile a wooden bridge, 7 yards long, spans a stream. At the 8th mile the bank of the Rongli is left and the road turns north up the valley of the Lingtam Chu. At 9 miles pass Lingtamtho, a clearing where a regiment could encamp, with a small collection of grass huts and a good water-supply, and ¾ mile on cross the Lingtam Chu by a single span wooden bridge 9 yards long and 5 feet in the clear ; the stream is ford-able, but the banks are steep. At 10½ miles the old road joins in from the left and the Keu Chu is crossed by a log bridge, 10 yards long with a 6-foot roadway ; stream unfordable. Here a stiff ascent, average gradient 1 in 10, commences for the next 2⅔ miles into camp. Keu village lies above and to the left (west) of the Keu Chu. At 12 miles pass Phaden-chen, a small hamlet of grass huts with a fair water-supply, situated on gently sloping ground in a clear-ing in the forest and at 13 miles reach Sedongchen, a scattered collection of some 30 bamboo mat houses.
				The rest-house, which stands above the village at an elevation of 6,500 feet, is a rough wooden building containing two small rooms. Water is carried to the bungalow in iron pipes, and hence is carried on in wooden troughs to the village below ; supply good and abundant. The camping-ground lies below the bungalow to the left of the road and is sufficient to accommodate half a regiment, but as it lies in a hollow into which the surface drainage of the ridge and village flows it could not be used after rain ; it is generally used as a picketing-ground by the numerous mule caravans passing through and would therefore require thorough cleaning before being employed by troops. Fodder (bamboo) obtainable on hill-sides below the village.
				No post or telegraph offices.
				The march is through dense jungle throughout and would be very trying to troops at any time except during the winter. The valley of the Rongli is very narrow and becomes excessively hot at mid-day.
6	GNATHONG	9½	73½	A steady ascent by a paved road, which in places is very bad, through forest which gradually becomes thinner and gives place to firs and rhododendrons as the summit of Lingtu is approached.
				At 2 miles pass Jeyluk, a dâk-runner's halting-place, consisting of two huts, one of stone and the other of matting, elevation 9,060 feet ; here there is a

Route No. 3—*concld.*

No. of stages.	Names of stages.	Distances.		Remarks.
		Inter-mediate.	Total.	
				considerable clearing in the forest. Above Jeyluk the ascent becomes very steep, the average being 1 in 7. At 3½ miles water is obtainable from a mountain torrent flowing to the right of the road. At 4½ miles reach Garnei, a single stone hut, here the new road round Lingtu turns off left, thus avoiding several hundred feet of climb over the summit of the hill; the new road rejoins the old track a mile on, but is narrow and rough, and is not passable before the middle of May owing to the heavy snow which lies in the *re-entrant* angles. The old road crosses the summit of Lingtu, elevation 12,617 feet. Hence to Gnathong the road is over undulating hill-sides and there are numerous ascents and descents of from 200 to 400 feet, but the gradients are easy. The last mile into Gnathong the road is very rough; hill-sides fairly open with here and there patches of fir forest and rhododendron.
				Fort Gnathong, elevation 12,030 feet, has now been destroyed, and the only building which remains is a small wooden dâk bungalow. To the south of the bungalow is a lake some 100 yards long drained by a considerable stream. Water-supply is a spring on the hill-side due south. There is ample space to the south of the fort on which to encamp troops. Fuel abundant from clumps of pine forest in the vicinity but no fodder. Hills in the vicinity are fairly open and gently sloping and rise some 800 feet higher than the fort itself. In addition to the dâk bungalow some 17 wooden huts, more or less in a state of disrepair, are still standing. They are used as wood-sheds by traders.
				The road is metalled in places and bridged throughout and is passable to infantry, baggage animals and mountain artillery without any difficulty.

Route No. 4.

From DARJEELING to GANTOK (*via* KALIMPONG, RHENOCK AND PAKYONG).

Authority and date.—ROUTES IN SIKKIM, 1894, AND CAPTAIN F. C. COLOMB, 42ND GURKHA RIFLES, SEPTEMBER 1895.

No. of stages.	Names of stages.	Distances.		Remarks.
		Inter-mediate.	Total.	
1—3	PASHOK KALIMPONG PADONG.	...	43	For Darjeeling to Padong, see Route No. 3.
4	PAKYONG . . .	15	58	To Rhenock Bazar, 5½ miles (see Route No. 3), hence the Gantok road branches off N.-W. It is generally in good condition, being well paved in all its steep ascents and descents. It is mostly cut in such hard stone as to render metalling unnecessary. Its average width is 7 feet, but when paving is laid down it has only a breadth of 4 feet. For the first 2 miles after leaving Rhenock the road is almost level and is cut through the cultivated slopes of a hill-side facing S.-W. A saddle is then crossed, and in the next 1½ miles the road drops about 1,000 feet to the Rungpo Chu, passing through thin jungle and patches of cultivation, gradients about $\frac{1}{13}$, road well paved and in excellent order, but very slippery after rain.

No. of stages.	Names of stages.	DISTANCES.		REMARKS.
		Inter-mediate.	Total.	
				The Rungpo Chu is a rapid stream flowing in a rocky bed through a valley which here opens ont into a considerable expanse of flat cultivated land which in the winter months would form an excellent camping ground sufficient for the requirements of a brigade. In summer it is covered with rice cultivation. The average elevation of this valley is 1,900 feet or 1,130 feet below Rhenock Bazar. The river is unfordable at all seasons of the year, it averages about 30 yards wide and has gently sloping banks. It is spanned by a wooden bridge on the cantilever system, 31 yards long, with a 7-foot roadway, 15 feet high above water level.
				Road now for ½ mile is along the flat valley; this portion becomes boggy in the rains when the adjoining stretches of cultivation are under irrigation. At 4 miles cross the Khani-Khola stream by a wooden bridge on the same principle as that above described; bridge is 20 yards long with a roadway 6 feet in the clear and 25 feet above high water level. The stream is unimportant and is fordable at all seasons, but its banks, above the bridge, are rocky and precipitous.
				The road now ascends the Pakyong spur by easy zigzags up which there are many short cuts; on the lower spurs there is thick bush and tree jungle which gives place to cultivation and clearings as the ascent is continued.
				At 12 miles pass Pachi-Khani a village of 50 or 60 bamboo and grass huts, lying to the right of and below the road; in the neighbourhood of the village are extensive copper mines; elevation of village 3,200 feet. For the next two miles the ascent is easy; the last mile into Pakyong is almost level. Half a mile short of Pakyong the road from Rungpo joins the road under report (*vide* Route No. 5).
				There is a scarcity of drinking water along the road between Rhenock Bazar and the Rungpo Chu, but beyond that it is plentiful at all seasons.
				Pakyong, elevation 4,600 feet, is situated on a saddle, the hill-slopes rising easily to either side; an extensive view is obtained towards Gantok and Rhenock. There is a good *bazar* containing several bunniahs' shops and a fair sized wooden house sufficient to accommodate 50 men. A market is held every Monday when fresh beef and pork and a small supply of vegetables may be purchased. The principal man here is a Newar called Lachmi Narayan, who can supply coolies, etc.
				Good stone dâk bungalow containing 3 furnished rooms with dressing-rooms. Along the ridge is a fairly level open stretch of ground where half a battalion could encamp if scattered. A better camp sufficient for one regiment is to be found to the west about ¼ mile distant up the hill towards the Kartok monastery, it is fairly level and measures 100 × 50 yards. The monastery is a good stone building of the usual pattern, well situated near the summit of the ridge, and commanding an extensive view towards the south and east. In front of it there is a level terrace about 50 yards square, and there are numerous smaller buildings round about. Water: there is a spring some 300 feet below the *bazar* and another at the dâk bungalow, but both furnish a very scanty supply and are liable to dry up between November and March. *Transport animals can, however, be watered at the small streams which cross the road from ½ mile to 1 mile from bungalow. Bamboo fodder is plentiful, and there is a little grazing for animals.
5	GANTOK . . .	10½	68½	From Pakyong the road descends to the Roro Chu at an even and fairly easy gradient; in its upper portion it passes over closely cultivated hill-sides dotted with small settlements, while in the vicinity of the valley bottoms there is tree jungle with thin undergrowth.

Route No. 4—*contd.*

No. of stages.	Names of stages.	Distances.		Remarks.
		Intermediate.	Total.	
				The road is throughout good. At 2½ miles cross the Nampe Chu, an unimportant stream flowing in a narrow valley through heavy forest, by a single span wooden bridge 7 yards long and 6 feet wide on stone piers; no hand rails. At 4 miles the Ronke Chu crossed by a single span wooden bridge, without hand rails, 10 yards long with a 6-foot roadway.
				The next ¾ mile the road is up the left bank of the Rongni Chu and is almost level passing at first through forest, then emerging on open cultivated flat where there is a small village. At 4½ miles the Taksom Chu or Singtam-Khola, a stream which is only fordable at the driest season of the year, is crossed by a strong, single span wooden bridge 13 yards long and 15 feet above high water level; elevation 2,880 feet. Hence the road is level, crossing a fair sized cultivated flat, where a brigade could encamp, to the Roro Chu. The stream is 19 yards wide, very rapid and flowing over large boulders, only fordable, and that with difficulty, at the driest season of the year. It is crossed by a single span iron truss bridge, 21 yards long with a 5-foot roadway, 14 feet above high water level. Elevation 3,000 feet.
				Hence the road gradually ascends through thin tree jungle to Gantok; it is in excellent order; metalled where the soil requires it, is 6 feet wide and has an average gradient of $\frac{1}{13}$. The trace has lately been considerably improved and the length of the march somewhat shortened.
				At 8½ miles a road turns off left to Darjeeling *viâ* Song and Namchi (*vide* Route No. 6) or to Pamionchi (*vide* Route No. 24).
				Gantok is the name given to a number of scattered habitations occupying some miles of the ridge and hillside south of and below the Intchi monastery. Since the location of troops a small *bazar* has sprung up north of and close to the Raja's palace, and between this *bazar* and the knoll occupied by the Intchi monastery is the station consisting of post and telegraph offices and dâk bungalow, officers' mess, and two other houses. The elevation of the *bazar* is about 5,900 feet, the lines are about 100 feet lower. Water is brought in from the valley towards the Penlong La, in 2½ inch iron pipes; the supply is unlimited at the head, but has to be conveyed in pipes some 2 miles to the station. The political officer has his residence on the west slope of the hills rather higher than the rest of the station, and north of, and about ⅓ mile distant from, the military lines.
				Gantok possesses camp accommodation for about two battalions of infantry if scattered, the best ground for this purpose being on the small flat round the palace and below, and to the east of the palace where there is a stretch of cultivation on fairly level ground. It would be difficult to camp troops at Gantok between the months of April and October owing to the enormous number of leeches which are found there. The Raja's palace is a strong stone building with walls 5 feet thick at their base; it consists of three stories, and is capable of holding 200 men; the roof is of sheet iron. Outside the palace is a piece of flat ground some 50 yards square.
				There is the following barrack accommodation. Two separate barracks, double storied, stone, iron roofs, Lansdowne pattern, slightly modified, each divided into four section rooms. The two barracks are for 2 companies, *i.e.*, 224 rank and file. Native officers' quarters; single storey, stone, iron roof, to hold 4 native officers. Hospital: Single storey, stone, iron roof, to hold 13 beds and containing Hospital Assistant's room, office, dispensary and godown. Followers lines are in course of construction.

Route No. 4—*concld.*

No. of stages.	Names of stages.	Distances.		Remarks.
		Inter-mediate.	Total.	
				Water-supply : five springs enclosed in stone upon the hill above the Residency about 500 feet above the barracks, brought down in pipes (iron) $1\frac{1}{2}''$ thick ; the barrack supply is led into a stone tank 8' square and containing 4' of water. Parade ground 96 × 75 yds. Cholera camp east of the *bazar* ridge 2,000' below it ; good water-supply ; no habitations near. Rations supplied by commissariat, no possibility of their being supplied otherwise.
				Transport animals can be camped on some flat ground below the Intchi Kazi's house, and can be watered from a small stream which crosses the road near this point. Bamboo fodder can be obtained in any quantity from along the new Lagyap road and elsewhere.
				From Gantok roads lead to Gnathong *viâ* Lagyap La, to Darjeeling *viâ* Rangit Bazar, Song and Namchi, and to the north of Sikkim *viâ* Tumlong.
				A *bazar* is held on Sundays when grain is procurable. Local supplies consist of Indian corn, salt from Tibet, and country vegetables. No supplies in any quantities are, however, procurable without early notice. Heliograph signalling is possible between Gantok and Jalapahar (distant 25 to 30 miles as the crow flies) in clear weather, which is generally only to be found from October to March.

Route No. 5.

From DARJEELING to GANTOK (*viâ* Rungpo).

Authority and date.—Captain W. F. O'Connor, R.G.A., 1900.

No. of stages.	Names of stages.	Distances.		Remarks.
		Inter-mediate.	Total.	
1	Teesta Bridge	$18\frac{1}{2}$	$18\frac{1}{2}$	For this stage see Route No. 3.
2	Rungpo	14	$32\frac{1}{2}$	Cross the Teesta by the suspension bridge described in Route No. 3. Follow the Kalimpong cart road for $\frac{1}{2}$ mile ; here the new cart road up the Teesta valley branches off. This is a good 12-foot road, unmetalled at present, running practically level for 14 miles to Rungpo. Numerous small side streams are crossed which are bridged by strong wooden bridges. The road runs through heavy jungle throughout along the left bank of the Teesta some few hundred feet above the level of the stream. At 3 miles reach Malighat. Here there is a small wooden two-roomed dak bungalow. The river can be crossed here during the cold weather in a dug-out canoe. Camping ground 120 feet square has been cleared of jungle. A larger area could be cleared if required.
				Riding path leads hence up the hill to Kalimpong Bazar.
				At 9 miles a path to the right leads up to Kalimpong a distance of 8 miles. For the first mile this path leads up the Tar Chu, which has to be forded three times ; stream 2 feet deep, current swift, bottom stony. For the next two miles the path rises steeply through forest, and then emerges on an open cultivated hill-side. Fair pathway for 4 miles further to crest of hill overlooking Kalimpong, whence $\frac{1}{2}$ miles descent and $\frac{1}{2}$ mile level into Kalimpong Bazar. A fair path ; passable for ponies or laden animals throughout.
				Following the cart-road from the 9th mile a camping ground similar to that described above is found at $10\frac{3}{4}$

Route No. 5.—concld.

No. of stages.	Names of stages.	DISTANCES.		REMARKS.
		Intermediate.	Total.	
				miles. The name of this place is Turang and there is a ferry here also during the cold weather. One mile short of the Rungpo the road has been blasted through a perpendicular cliff over-hanging the river. At 14 miles reach the bank of the Rungpo Chu which is crossed by a light suspension bridge of 270 feet span capable of taking laden animals. The stream itself can be forded for 10 months in the year, as the water is only 1½ to 2½ feet deep and the river bed smooth and gravelly. On the further side lies Rungpo Bazar, a collection of some 10 or 12 bamboo shanties where a very small quantity of supplies may be obtained, chiefly Indian corn. The dâk bungalow lies just beyond and above the *bazar*: it is a small, wooden, 3-roomed house with the necessary furniture. Limited camping ground near the bungalow. Another spot suitable for camping near the river about 400 yards square. Water and bamboo fodder plentiful. A large well-kept orange orchard just behind the bungalow. A path leads from here up the left bank of the Teesta to Tokul passing Katong, and connecting Routes No. 5, 6, and 7, distance about 7½ miles. This is a fair path and ponies can be taken along it, but in several places it is too narrow for a laden animal to pass. At 2 miles Katong flat is reached (see Route No. 7) half a mile beyond which is the ferry. Here Route No. 7 is crossed. Hence to Tokul is 5½ miles, the path running at an average height of about 100 feet above the river through forest and cultivation, and 1 mile from Tokul the Rongni Chu, or Singtam Khola, is crossed by a strong wooden cantilever bridge, 100 feet span 4-foot roadway, strong enough to take laden animals. The stream, during the rains, is unfordable. Ground in the neighbourhood of the mouth of the stream where it joins the Teesta level and open. This would make a good camping ground if the grass jungle were cleared. At 7½ miles Tokul bungalow for which see Route No. 6.
3	PAKYONG	9½	42	A long steady pull up a winding 6-foot track for 3½ miles to where Route No. 7 joins the road under report at the turning off to Duga, which lies ¼ mile off up the hill to the left; hence level for ½ mile, and then descend slightly to cross a small stream by a strong wooden bridge, whence steady rise to crest of hill over Pakyong at 8 miles. Road runs through rice and maize cultivation throughout. On the crest of the ridge there is a fair camping ground; enough for two battalions at a push; pasture fair; good water supply ¼ mile down the road towards Pakyong. Hence easy descent of 1 mile to join Rhenock-Pakyong road ½ mile from Pakyong dâk bungalow, for which see Route No. 4.
4	GANTOK	10½	52½	For this stage see Route No. 4.

Route No. 6.

From DARJEELING to GANTOK (*via* MANJHITAR BAZAR, NAMCHI AND SONG).

Authority and date.—BRIGADIER-GENERAL YEATMAN-BIGGS, C.B., 1896; AND CAPTAIN W. F. O'CONNOR, R.G.A., 1900.

No. of stages	Names of stages.	DISTANCES.		REMARKS.
		Intermediate.	Total.	
1	MANJHITAR BAZAR	11	11	Leaving Darjeeling there are two roads as far as Lebong; one runs steeply down from the chowrasta elevation 7,010 feet, passes through "Bhutia basti"

No. of stages.	Names of stages.	DISTANCES.		REMARKS.
		Inter-mediate.	Total.	
				at ¾ mile, and meets the cart-road 2 miles below Darjeeling. It is a steep road, having a gradient of ⅛ in places, but is quite practicable for laden animals; average width 8 feet. The other road is a first-class metalled cart-road (a continuation in fact of the railway road) running from the Darjeeling station through the *bazar*, round Birch hill, passing St. Joseph's college at Singamari (here a side road to Singla turns off to the left, see Route No. 8), and joining the road from the chowrasta just above Lebong, elevation 6,000 feet. This road continues to Lebong, distance 4¼ miles from Darjeeling.
				The road down to the Rangit turns off to the right from the big cart-road ⅛ mile short of Lebong, and passes the Darjeeling and Ging tea companies gardens. At 6 miles Badamtam tea factory is passed (3,333 feet), and ¾ mile further on is the Badamtam dâk bungalow, a good 3-roomed stone bungalow, where, however, there is little or no camping ground, as the bungalow is surrounded by forest, with tea growing just below. Road continues to descend through forest until at 8 miles it reaches the crest of the spur. The old road to Rangit, or Jalung, Bazar now runs to the right; it can be followed to the bank of the Rangit river (10th mile) whence a track (formerly a cart-road) leads along the right bank of the river to the junction of the Rangit with the Teesta (see Route No. 3). The new road to Manjhitar Bazar is a good track, 4 to 5 feet in width, carried down the face of the spur through forest at an easy gradient for 3 miles to the river bank opposite the *bazar*. From this spot roads run up and down the Rangit.
				The road running up the right bank reaches Singla Bazar at 3 miles; it is a narrow 3-foot track, level, running through forest, practicable for baggage animals. 200 yds. from where it leaves the Badamtam road it crosses the Jhebi Khola, a wide shallow stream easily fordable except after heavy rain. This path joins Route No. 8 at Singla.
				The road which runs down the right bank joins the old Rangit valley road at 1 mile. It is a good 4-foot track, level, and fit for passage of baggage animals.
				A suspension bridge is now in course of construction at Manjhitar. This bridge will have a span of 560 feet. At present the river can be crossed in a dug-out canoe. There are 2 of these canoes worked by boatmen on the spot. They are each about 40 feet long, 2½ feet wide, sides 2½ feet high. They can carry 12 to 15 persons at a time. The river is about 120 yeards in width, and quite unfordable; current very swift. Animals can however be swum across except immediately after heavy rain. Ferry rates 1 pice per passenger, or maund of baggage.
				Manjhitar Bazar stands on the left bank of the Rangit immediately above the ferry. It is a long straggling street of some 30 or 40 bamboo huts, mostly shops kept by Hindu merchants. Twenty or 30 maunds of rice could probably be procured on the spot, and also a considerable quantity of Indian corn. The latter could be provided in practically unlimited quantities on a few days' notice. There is a post office here but no rest house. Camping ground limited and dirty. Space could probably be found for a mountain battery or battalion of infantry if scattered. Water from the river. Bamboo fodder.
2	NAMCHI . . .	7	18	Leaving Manjhitar Bazar the road runs through forest for 3½ miles to Keitam rising gradually at an easy gradient for the first 2 miles, and hence more steeply to the village of Keitam; average width of road about 6 feet. About one mile short of Keitam there is a piece of ground sufficient to encamp two companies in a sheltered position with a limited water-supply. Keitam is a village of 50 houses, 3½ miles from the Rangit

Route No. 6—*contd.*

No. of stages.	Names of stages.	DISTANCES.		REMARKS.
		Inter-mediate.	Total.	
				bridge, elevation 2,575 feet, situated on a dry, healthy spur, water from a spring a quarter of a mile beyond the village; a market is held here on Fridays, but no supplies in any quantity are available. Mika, which is a sub-division of Keitam, is passed 1½ miles on; elevation 4,000 feet; no supplies and no accommodation.
				From Mika a new road has been cut, 6 feet wide with a gradient ₁/₁₅ along the hill-side to the saddle below Namchi.
				Namchi, elevation 5,608 feet, occupies the crest of a low-lying saddle on the spur below Tendong. Village possesses about 100 head of cattle and a considerable supply of food-grains. On the right hand side, about 200 feet up the spur, lies the Namchi monastery, and on the left, about 300 yards from the road, is the dâk bungalow, in the vicinity of which accommodation for about two companies is available; a third company could camp in scattered parties on the ledges of ground sloping to the north and east. Water for transport animals would be brought from the stream below the road. There is small *bazar* of half a dozen shops where supplies in small quantities can be procured.
				There is extensive cultivation both above and below the road throughout the stage, though the slopes of the hills are steep and stony. Between Keitam and Namchi, forest has been entirely cleared off the hills. From Namchi two paths run down to the Rangit; one to Singla Bazar, where there is at present no bridge (see Route No. 8), and the other to a suspension bridge which crosses the Rangit ½ mile above the junction of the Rammam (see Route No. 8). These are both good paths, fit for animals; and the latter is at present the only route by which animals can be brought from Namchi to Darjeeling or *vice versâ.*
3	TEMI , . . .	8½	26½	Road 4 feet wide, ascending at an easy gradient skirting the hill along the southern slope with precipitous *khuds* on the left hand side, water abundant. Road then ascends at a steeper gradient for about 2½ miles, and turning abruptly to the right crosses the ridge connecting the Tendong and Rufu La peaks and leaving Damthang, elevation 5,540 feet, half a mile off the road on the left. From here the road to Pamionchi turns off to the left (*vide* Route No. 24). Road now through heavy forest; rocky and liable to be carried away by slips during the rains; ascent is gentle. At 1½ miles a steep descent commences, gradient ⅕, a north-easterly spur of Tendong being followed. The dense forest continues for about 2 miles and suddenly terminates, when the road emerges on the highest fields of Temi at an elevation of 5,400 feet, the village lying to the left of the road. Here one company could encamp were the jungle cleared; water is limited and 300 or 400 yards distant.
				Hence a road leads to Barmie monastery, distant 3½ miles east; it is a fair track and is rideable throughout, except in a few places, where rocks require blasting. Altitude of Barmie, 5,100 feet.
4	SONG	11	37½	From Temi the road descends to the village of Turko, altitude 3,000 feet, passing Chowbo half way; soil clay or loam the whole way, and very slippery after rain. The greater part of this road has now been metalled. Turko is on the right hand side of the road, the houses being scattered and few; from the roadway itself the village is scarcely visible. From Turko the road descends steeply through dense jungle and undergrowth, swarming with leeches in the rains, for about 1½ miles in zigzags, slope at times is as much as 12°. At the foot of the descent the Teesta river is reached, the stream in the rains being 100 yards in width and quite unfordable. Follow the right bank down for ½ mile to where the old bridge existed which was washed

Route No. 6—*concld.*

No. of stages.	Names of stages.	Distances.		Remarks.
		Inter-mediate.	Total.	
				away some years ago. On the far side of the river (left bank) is a small village called Lingtsi. Accommodation available here for half a battalion of infantry and a mountain battery; elevation 1,460 feet. From Lingtsi the old road ascends steeply at slopes of from 12° to 18° up the south-west spur from Ganam, averaging 6 feet in width and becoming less steep as the upper slopes are reached. Water is plentiful all along the route.
				On reaching the bottom of the hill, a new road has been made along the right bank of the Teesta to the new bridge at Tokul, which has a 225 feet span and a 4-foot roadway; distance 2½ miles along bank of river. At Tokul there is a poor camping-ground on left bank, a small *bazar* and a rest-house containing 2 small rooms. From Tokul the new road zigzags up the hill and joins the old one ¼ mile before reaching Song bungalow.
				From Tokul a road runs along the Teesta to Rungpo junction, 7½ miles. *Vide* Route No. 5.
				Song consists of many scattered houses extending all over the southern and western slopes of Ganam, where much ground is cultivated and oranges largely grown. On the right hand side of the road near some " chaits " (monuments) is the dâk bungalow.
5	Gantok . . .	15	52½	Road ascends slightly and skirts the slopes of Ganam and Phambong, passing Murtam at 5 miles, average width 6 feet. It now turns north and becoming steeper ascends for 3 miles to Ramthek. Here a considerable number of men could encamp in scattered parties; water abundant and bamboo fodder easily obtainable; a limited number of coolies procurable. There is a stone monastery in good condition. Road now due north and level for a mile, when it descends steeply to the river Rahni at a gradient of ⅛, the roadway being 6 to 8 feet wide. The foot of the hill is reached at five miles, forest being passed through, and the river is crossed by a wire rope bridge about 50 feet long and 3 feet wide. Hence an ascent at first at a gradient of ¼ and latterly at ⅛ for about 2¼ miles where the main road to Gantok (*vide* Route No. 4) is joined. For the next 2 miles the road is 7 feet wide and winds up the spur at a slope of 4° to 6°. Reaching Gantok the road becomes almost level. For Gantok, see Route No. 4.

Route No. 7.

From DARJEELING to GANTOK (*viâ* Sedam).

Authority and date.—Capt. W. F. O'Connor, R. G. A., 1900.

No. of stages.	Names of stages.	Distances.		Remarks.
		Inter-mediate.	Total.	
1	Manjhitar bazar .	11	11	For this stage see Route No. 6.
2	Sedam . . .	8	19	From Manjhitar Bazar keep along the Namchi road for 3 miles; then turn off to the right and follow a fairly level road to Manpur Khola, at 4½ miles. Hence 1½ miles steep rise to Turuk, where there is a small village, and the residence of a wealthy Nepali, Lachmi Das, who is a man of considerable local influence, and could collect coolies or supplies. He keeps a room here for the use of travellers. Hence 2 miles steep rise to Sedam, where there is a small *bazar*, and a Mission house, where travellers can be lodged. No proper camping ground. Practically no supplies, although a little

Route No. 7—*concld.*

No. of stages.	Names of stages.	DISTANCES.		REMARKS.
		Intermediate.	Total.	
				Indian corn and rice might be collected. Water-supply plentiful from streams. Bamboo fodder. The road throughout is a good 4 to 5 feet track, passable for baggage animals.
3	NAMTON	8	27	The road from Sedam runs at an easy gradient along the hill-side for 8 miles to Namton (or Namthang); several small streams are crossed, but they offer no difficulties, gradients easy. At Namton there is a collection of a few bamboo huts and a room for travellers. Supplies practically *nil.* No proper camping ground. Water and fodder abundant. Road good and practicable for animals.
4	DUGA	7½	34½	Road rises from Namton for a short distance to the summit of the ridge leaving the twin peaks of Tameok on the right. Hence steep descent of some 3,000 feet through forest to the Teesta river at 4 miles. Here the river can be crossed during the cold weather in a dug-out canoe; during the rains the crossing is dangerous and is not used by the natives. The ferry is called Budang Ghat, or sometimes Katong Ghat. Width of river 100 yards. The current is swift and deep, and the river is never fordable. Crossing the river a path is found running along the left bank of the Teesta (see Route No. 5). Follow this path to the right for ⅔ mile skirting the large fertile plain of Katong. This is a stretch of rice cultivation about ⅔ mile by ½ mile, dotted with houses, and lying about 150 feet above the river. There is excellent level camping ground here on firm grassy land for a battalion of infantry or a mountain battery. Wood, water, and fodder abundant. The path to Duga now turns north up the hill through forest for 1½ miles to a village of "Kamis" or smiths, where a great deal of copper smelting is done. Hence 2 miles steady rise through rice and maize cultivation to the small hamlet of Duga situated on a saddle of the ridge. Here there is a little 2-roomed wooden bungalow for the accommodation of travellers. It is the property of a Nepali named Lachmi Narayan who lives at Kalimpong. Good camping ground for a battalion near by. Water-supply scanty but good, from a spring 200 yards below the bungalow. A little Indian corn procurable locally; otherwise no supplies. Bamboo fodder plentiful. This last section of the road from the river up to Duga is very narrow in places; but is practicable for animals.
5	PAKYONG	7¼	41¾	Path from Duga level for ¼ mile, then steep descent (¼) for ½ mile to join Rungpo-Pakyong road 6½ miles from Pakyong. Hence to Pakyong see Route No. 5.
6	GANTOK	10½	52¼	For this stage see Route No. 4.

Route No. 8.

FROM DARJEELING TO PAMIONCHI (*via* SINGLA BAZAR, CHAKANG, AND RINCHENPONG).

Authority and date.—LIEUT. W. F. O'CONNOR, R.A., 1896; POLITICAL OFFICER IN SIKKIM, 1897.

No. of stages.	Names of stages.	DISTANCES.		REMARKS.
		Intermediate.	Total.	
1	CHAKANG	17	17	Follow the cart road from Darjeeling as far as St. Joseph's College at Singamari. Here turn off to the left and follow a road which runs steeply down hill to Singla

No. of stages.	Names of stages.	DISTANCES.		REMARKS.
		Inter-mediate.	Total.	
				Bazar on the great Rangit river; the road follows generally the crest of the Takvaar spur, and is a good 8-foot road, steepest gradient ½, running at first through forest, and afterwards through tea gardens down to the river, distance 11 miles.
				Three miles from Singamari the road forks; the right hand one being the road under report, that to the left following the crest of another spur down to the Little Rangit (see Route No. 10).
				Singla is a fair sized *bazar* where coolies from the neighbouring tea gardens get most of their supplies. At present there is no bridge across the Rangit here, as the old bridge has been dismantled and removed; but a new one will probably be constructed this year (1900). A good path runs up the opposite hill-side to Namchi (see Route No. 6).
				The road to Chakang turns west from Singla, and follows the bank of the Great Rangit for about ½ mile, when the Little Rangit is crossed by a wire rope suspension bridge 120 ft. span. Continue along the right bank of the Great Rangit for 1 mile to the Rammam river which is crossed by a wire rope suspension bridge 180 ft. span and hence zig-zag steeply up the hill to Chakang bungalow on the summit of the ridge, 6 miles from Singla.
				Half way between the Little Rangit and Rammam rivers a path (fit for animals) turns west up the Gokh spur joining Route No. 10 higher up.
				After crossing the Rammam a path leads off to the right to a bridge across the Great Rangit 1 mile above the junction of the Great Rangit and Rammam rivers. This is a light suspension footway, similar to that at Rungpo (see Route No. 5), capable of taking laden animals. Hence a path leads up to Namchi (see Route No. 6).
				Chakang is a good 3-roomed bungalow with servants' quarters, stables, etc.; supplies *nil*; fuel, fodder, and water abundant. Camping space limited; there is room for a section of a mountain battery or 2 companies. Elevation, 5,190 feet.
				A good level road runs from here along the northern face of the hill to Seriong 4 miles, see Route No. 10.
2	RINCHENPONG	9	26	Down a steep slope north-east from the bungalow to a small stream, across which there is a rough foot-bridge, stream no obstacle to ponies or mules; then turn north up the hill-side and cross ridge after a climb of about 1,000 feet. Down steeply the other side, cross small stream and up the saddle of spur thrown out from Helu peak. From this point a new road runs north-west to Dentam, meeting Route No. 10 at Hi at distance of 8 miles; it is almost level, and streams are bridged. Road to Rinchenpong turns north-east from this saddle and runs round northern slopes of spur almost level to the dâk bungalow, which is situated near the summit. Road good all the way, though gradients in early part are steep. Bungalow is formed from a native house, well roofed and floored, with doors and windows let in, 2 large rooms, and 2 smaller ones; small monastery 500 yards away of usual pattern. Hill-side well cultivated; but in neighbourhood of bungalow open and grassy. Here troops could be camped, but water-supply is scanty. Fuel plentiful; bamboo fodder can be brought from a short distance. Supplies *nil*. Elevation of bungalow, 5,510 feet.
3	PAMIONCHI	11	37	General direction north; easy slope at first, then steep down to the Kulhait Chu, a considerable stream which is here bridged by strong bridge of sâl timber

Route No. 8—*concld.*

No. of stages.	Names of stages.	DISTANCES.		REMARKS.
		Inter-mediate.	Total.	
				50 feet in length with 5-foot roadway. Turn right after crossing bridge and in ½ mile reach junction of Kulhait with Great Rangit. Follow right bank of Rangit for ⅜ mile, when new iron bridge on Pamionchi-Gantok road is reached (*vide* Route No. 24). Hence road zig-zags sharply up hill to crest of spur, which it follows until Pamionchi Bazar is reached. This *bazar* is held on a flat some 200 yards square, close to where there is a very large Mendong or sacred wall, about 1½ miles below the monastery. *Bazar* day Friday.
				Road up to this in good condition, but steep and trying. Hence steep pull to dâk bungalow, passing below monastery. Bungalow is on crest of ridge, 3 rooms. Monastery, the most important in Sikkim, ¼ mile distant on highest point of ridge, which is a spur running out from Lampheram: a large square stone-building, of usual pattern, surrounded by many smaller out-buildings of better class than is usual, being mostly built of stone. Monastery has a fine situation and commands magnificent view in every direction, being plainly visible from Darjeeling in clear weather. A little further on down the crest of the ridge at Rubdentse are ruins of former Rajah's palace, which was evidently of considerable size. The only building left standing at present is a large square stone house, used as a cattleshed; it is in good condition and could be easily repaired and made habitable. There is some flat ground here where a small number of troops might be camped. Water from a small stream running close by. The whole of this large spur, and the valley of the Kulhait Chu generally, are very thickly populated, the hill-sides being covered with cultivation. There are numerous paths and tracks running from Pamionchi in every direction to other monasteries and farm-houses. Some of these will be found reported on elsewhere (see Routes 39 to 42). At an important centre like this one would expect to find some sort of village, but nothing of the kind exists: the buildings round the monastery being the only collection of houses in the district, and they of course are reserved for monks (*tabas*) and Lamas, who are nearly all Bhutias. Timber plentiful along crest and northern slopes of ridge. Bamboo fodder. Supplies as usual *nil*, except perhaps on *bazar* days, when some Indian corn and a little rice might be procured.
				Elevation of bungalow, 6,900 feet.

Route No. 9.

From DARJEELING to CHIABHANJAN (*via* the Nepal Frontier Road).

Authority and date.—Sikkim Routes, 1894; Lieut. W. F. O'Connor, R. A., 1896; and Brigadier-General Yeatman-Biggs, C.B., 1896.

No. of stages.	Names of stages.	DISTANCES.		REMARKS.
		Inter-mediate.	Total.	
1	Joe Pokri	12	12	The road first follows the Darjeeling-Himalayan Railway for about 4 miles as far as Ghoom Station. The Nepal frontier road then turns off to the right behind the station, and there is a slight descent for 1 mile (there is also a bridle path which turns off to the right

No. of stages.	Names of stages.	DISTANCES.		REMARKS.
		Inter- mediate.	Total.	
				through the Ghoom Bazar just short of the station and joins the main road at 1 mile from Ghoom, passing the Ghoom Monastery). Hence the road ascends gradually till, at 4 miles from Ghoom, the village of Sungri is reached. Good road all the way fit for field artillery; ½ of a mile further on pass "Ghoom Rock," which is the highest point on this section of the road. At 4½ miles from Ghoom there is a small village on the crest of the ridge, whence two paths lead down to the right, one going to the forest bungalow, Lepcha Jagat, and the other to Pul Bazar and the Little Rangit river. At 7 miles from Ghoom reach Sukia Pokri, where there is a large *bazar*, *bazar* day Friday, and where the Nepalese assemble in considerable numbers to supply the neighbouring gardens with coolies. Here there is a police thana and a post and telegraph office. At the west end of the *bazar* the road to Jor Pokri dâk bungalow branches off to the right, and leads to the bungalow along the crest of the ridge, the main road continuing to the left. The bungalow has 3 good rooms and is well fitted up. The road is good all the way, and has no steep gradients. During the rains it is a good deal cut up by cart traffic. Water-supply scanty.
				Elevation of dâk bungalow, 7,400 feet.
2	TONGLU . . .	10	22	Bridle path from the bungalow down to the cart-road which it joins near Simana. Here the cart-road terminates. Two roads lead onwards; the one to the left going to Merrik (or Mirig) in Nepal, 15 miles further on, and that to the right to Tonglu. The first Nepalese boundary stone is at the fork of the roads, and also a small village. The Tonglu road descends rapidly by a series of zig-zags for 1½ miles to Mani-Bhanjan whence three tracks diverge; that to the left leads to Ilam in Nepal, the centre one to Tonglu, and the right hand one is a forest path. The road now leads up a steep zig-zag to a village called Chittri between the 13th and 14th mile-stones. Here there is a fine open grassy knoll, where 500 men could be encamped if spread about. There is a moderate water-supply from a spring on the Nepal side of the hill.
				From Chittri about 4 miles of fairly level road, through a bamboo jungle and 1 mile of sharp ascent brings you to Tonglu, 10 miles from Jor Pokri, and almost at the 19th mile-stone. Thus far the road is very good and recently repaired. No bridges or culverts, except on the cart-road to Simana, on which section they are all first rate. Nearly the whole road is through forest. Water is scarce in dry seasons. There is good camping-ground at Tonglu for a brigade; fair water-supply at ordinary times, but small in dry weather. Water at forester's house ¼ mile, British side, and at a pond on Nepal side. Good three-roomed bungalow; very large iron-roofed stable, and good police bungalow. From here a foot path leads to Ilam and other places in Nepal. The trees here are webbiana, jaxus, juniper, birch, mountain ash, and 5 sorts of rhododendron.
				Elevation, 10,074 feet.
3	SANDAKPHU . . .	13	35	At the 19th mile-stone is a forest bungalow, which stands on a small spur. There is a spring in the ravine on each side a little way down.
				At 21 miles the road to Ilam, etc., turns off to the left at a long "mendong" or praying place, the road winding down a spur of a pointed hill called Thumka.
				At 21½ miles there is water, and just beyond 22 miles a good stream with abundant water. From Thumka the road runs down a wooded hill at a sharp zig-zag to a neck at about the 24th mile. The road is shady and good for mules, and water is abundant. At the

Route No. 9—*concld.*

No. of stages.	Names of stages.	DISTANCES.		REMARKS.
		Inter-mediate.	Total.	
				24th mile there is a steep zig-zag ascent. Just beyond the 28th mile-stone is the Kali Pokri (black pool), a fair sized tank of decent water, enough for a brigade. The tank is on the top of the ridge at Nepal pillar No. 13. From Kali Pokri the road ascends by a very irregular zig-zag over a sharp ridge (a short cut goes to the left) for ¼ mile, and then down a sharp descent on the other side. Over the ridge the vegetation suddenly changes, and there are quantities of picea, webbiana, and rhododendron campbellii. The road about here is very bad and rough, though passable for mules. At the 31st mile-stone there is a flat, and then a sharp rugged stony rise to Sandakphu, 32¼ miles. Water is very scarce on this ridge.
				There is a road into Nepal from this point. Scenery very wild. In dry weather the water-supply is very bad. One spring, Nepal side, below bungalow. A catchment basin is required.
				Elevation of dâk bungalow, 11,930 feet.
4	PHALLUT	13	48	The road is good and fairly level, no steep gradients. Ground open and bare, and there is a very poor water-supply. The road runs mainly through open forests of silver fir and rhododendron with occasional bare grassy places. At a little beyond 39th mile-stone is a deep valley with a stream of excellent water, which was running well at the end of an exceptionally dry season. This is half way. The name of the stream is Siri Khola. At the 41st mile-stone there is a conspicuous bare hill called Subarkum; elevation 11,640 feet. Here the main Nepal trade route crosses the ridge, and runs down to Rimbick, etc. It is much worn. The road now runs along a series of knife edges with magnificent wooded valleys on each side. At 45 miles Phallut. The bungalow is comfortable with a good stable. The hill is very bare and the country bleak and wild. Water-supply poor.
				Elevation of bungalow, 11,810 feet.
5	CHIABHANJAN	6	54	From Phallut there is a drop of 400 feet, steep but fairly easy to a col, and thence a very steep and difficult ascent to Singalela. The road is bad, at times almost dangerous. Singalela (12,130 feet) is the highest point on the road. Thence the road descends and passes along a very narrow col, not more than 3 feet wide in places, with a dense growth of rhododendron on either side. On passing the col the road runs on the east side of the hill, then crosses an open space and runs down the side of the spur to Chiabhanjan at the 51st mile-stone. Last 3 miles road very bad; gradient easy. Dâk bungalow of 3 rooms with furniture, servants' quarters, and stables. There is a large deep pool of water close to Chiabhanjan bungalow, difficult of access for animals at present, but a track could easily be made. The water is not fit for men's use. There is a spring at the bungalow.
				Elevation of bungalow, 10,320 feet.
				NOTE.—After leaving Phallut, and near No 1 boundary pillar, the road bears to the left to Nepal to Chung-Thap, Kabali Bazar, and a new Military station Tapli-Jong. It is No 5 station. There are 12 of these posts from Katmandu, which is No. 1 (the British frontier station at Ilam is independent of these); each of these stations has 3 out-posts. Tapli-Jong was newly formed in 1896. This chain of posts runs along the Tibet frontier. They are rebuilding barracks and go-downs
				From here 3 roads branch off; one east to Pamionchi, *via* Dentam (*vide* Route No. 41), one north along the crest of the ridge to Jongri and the Gamothang Lake District (*vide* Route No. 44), and the third west to Chang-thap in Nepal.

Route No. 10.

From DARJEELING to CHIABHANJAN (*viâ* Gokh and Dentam).

Authority and date.—Sikkim Routes, 1894; Lieut. W. F. O'Connor, R. A., 1896; Political Officer, Sikkim, 1897.

No. of stages	Names of stages.	Intermediate	Total.	Remarks.
1	Gokh	11	11	Road runs down Takvaar spur from Singamari on the new cart-road to Lebong. Three miles down it forks (*vide* Route No. 8). Take left hand road and descend through tea gardens to Little Rangit. Cross river by narrow wire suspension bridge, which sways considerably; river fordable except during the rains. Road generally good, gradients easy. Ascend steeply for about 2 miles to summit of Gokh ridge. Hence a path runs down the crest to Great Rangit river (*vide* Route No. 8). Road runs west, descending very steeply to valley of Rammam river through jungle. Road hither from Little Rangit, narrow and stony. The valley of the Rammam is here open and level. Troops could be camped in the fields. Water from river. Bamboo fodder from jungle. No supplies. This valley is inhabited chiefly by Nepalese, who possess a good many cows, goats, and sheep.
2	Seriong	8	19	Road level along right bank of Rammam through open cultivated valley for about 3 miles. Cross the stream by a wooden bridge;* current rapid; stream fordable except when in flood. Hence ascend by a good bridle path to Seriong, gradient at first easy, growing steeper near the top of the ridge; hill-sides cultivated and open. From Seriong good level road east to Chakang, 4 miles. Small *bazar* of 6 shops at Seriong. Small quantities of rice and maize procurable; water, fuel, and fodder abundant.
3	Dentam	12	31	Road from Seriong winds along the hill-sides for about 3 miles, and enters forest land at an elevation of 5,300 feet. Hence the path runs through forest for some 7 miles as far as Hi village clearing, when the road from Rinchenpong joins road under report (see Route No. 8). Hence to Dentam 2 miles; road nearly level. Dentam is a broad tract of rice cultivation on the right bank of the Kulhait Chu. There is space for 3 regiments to encamp when the fields are dry. Water, fodder, and fuel abundant. There is a 4-roomed dâk bungalow, built of stone with sheet-iron roof. Elevation 4500 feet. Hence road to Pamionchi (*vide* Route No. 41). *N.B.*—The track through the forest between Seriong and Hi is a narrow path along which ponies can be led. Some repairs would be necessary before laden animals could be taken over it.
4	Chiabhanjan	8	39	Path up right bank of Kulhait Chu. Cross two streams by wooden bridges. Banks of streams thickly wooded, hill-sides otherwise bare. Road leaves banks of stream and ascends hill-side steeply to Mongthang plateau, which extends for about 2 miles, when Kulhait Chu is again reached and steep ascent commences, which lasts right up to Chiabhanjan, through narrow valley with steep wooded hills on either side; cross the Kulhait by a wooden bridge, and ascend steeply to summit of small ridge. From here the road turns right and makes a long zig-zag to summit of ridge, passing through dense bamboo and rhododendron jungle. There is a very steep short cut to the bungalow. Road fair throughout and passable to laden mules. For description of bungalow and other roads leading thither, see Route No. 9.

* This bridge has been washed away; there is at present a temporary foot-way (September 1900).

Route No. 11.

From DARJEELING to SAMATEK (via Namchi and Teesta Valley Road).

Authority and date.—Sikkim Route Book, 1894; Political Officer, Sikkim, 1897.

No. of stages.	Names of stages.	DISTANCES.		REMARKS.
		Inter-mediate.	Total.	
1 to 3	TEMI	26½	26½	Follow Route No. 6 as far as Temi.
4	NAMPUK	9	35½	Follow Route No. 6 as far as the Teesta : here instead of turning south to the new bridge, turn north up the right bank of the river, crossing the Rimpi Chu, which is fordable except after heavy rain. From the Rimpi Chu to the Rungpo Chu is a level ¾-mile over cultivation.
				The Rungpo Chu is fordable, but a ricketty bamboo bridge exists, which is only used when the stream is in flood. Hence road level for ¼ mile over rice fields, after which there is a sharp ascent of one mile over a bad and rocky bit to some fields, altitude 1,900 feet, when ascent becomes easy and gradual on a good gravelly road for 2½ miles to the usual camping-ground of Nampuk, which is a collection of villages on the slope of the hill east of Yangong monastery. Camping-ground good, and water plentiful. Elevation, 2,400 feet. The Teesta Valley is very hot and infested with "pipsa," but there are no leeches anywhere under 3,000 feet.
5	BHOMSONG	8	43½	A difficult march owing to numerous ascents and descents, and to the great heat in the valley of the Teesta and in the several lateral nullahs which are crossed, all of which are of a tropical character. From Nampuk the road keeps level and good for ½ mile, then descends for ¼ mile to the Rungum Chu, a stream, altitude 2,000 feet, which is crossed by a ricketty bridge. It then ascends to Neh Mendong, 1 mile, altitude 2,700 feet; this ascent is particularly bad, rocky, steep and narrow, and is not passable to transport animals; no water at Neh Mendong. This Mendong is famous as being the place where the Gurkhas were driven back from their conquest of Sikkim in 1787. Gigantic cliffs extend from this spot to Moinam rock, altitude 9,900 feet. The Lepchas and Bhutias made this a strong defensive position and hurled down enormous rocks on the invaders, who were compelled to retreat with heavy loss.
				The road now descends ½ mile to the Sungkum Nala which is dry in the hot season, then ascends 2 miles to Lingmo Mendong, altitude 3,250 feet. Two pure springs of water are passed on the road ½ mile beyond Sungkum Nala. With the exception of ½ mile of good road the rest of this last 2½ miles of path is a mere narrow rocky track unfit for laden mules, but rideable with a good hill pony. No water at Lingmo Mendong. From here the road is in good order and descends gradually for ¾ mile to Kossair Mendong, altitude 2,900 feet, where there is a small spring of water. Two more miles of descent over a fair but stony road, and the Teesta river is reached at Bhomsong Samdong, altitude 1,480 feet. Just before reaching the river the Runnett Chu is crossed.
				Hence a road crosses the Teesta and leads to Tumlong, *via* Nampung, 2 marches, 23 miles, joining the Gantok-Tumlong road before it crosses the Dik Chu. The Teesta is crossed by a cane bridge which is kept up for local use and is often in a rotten condition. The Teesta here is almost always impassable for ponies, except in the middle of the cold weather, when they have to be dragged across by ropes. Road is only used locally by foot passengers. (*Vide* Route No. 22, Stage 1.)
6	LINGTIAM	6	49½	Road along right bank of Teesta for 1½ miles to the junction of the Rumphap river, up which it turns for ¼ mile. On leaving the Rumphap stream a very steep ascent to the village of Lingtiam, 3¾ miles; altitude 4,400 feet.

Route No. 11—*concld.*

No. of stages.	Names of stages.	Distances.		Remarks.
		Inter-mediate.	Total.	
7	Ralung Ghat . .	10	59½	Path leads over some fine cliffs to the Sandang spur and Mendong, 3 miles, altitude 5,050 feet ; thence descends to the Pi Chu river, 2 miles below the village of Gourh. From here there is a short ascent over a precipice followed by a descent of 3 miles to the junction of a small stream with the Teesta, then level for a mile along the bank of the river to the camping-ground at the cane bridge over the Teesta at Ralung Ghat. Elevation, 1,650 feet.
8	Maling . . .	8	67½	Cross by the cane bridge to the left bank of the Teesta and follow bank for 4 miles to the junction of the Rongrong Chu, then an ascent of ¼ mile over a precipice ; road here bad and dangerous. From the summit of the cliff a gentle ascent to the village of Dapia or Tugyia, elevation 3,200 feet ; hence road ascends to the Ringon spur for 1 mile, whence it is fairly level to Maling, 2 miles further on.
				Ralung crossing almost always impassable for ponies.
				These last three marches are impassable for ponies and hardly to be called a road.
9	Samatek . . .	8(?)	75½	Road from here runs up a spur to the new Tumlong-Samatek road, meeting it about 1½ miles from Samatek. (See Route No. 22, Stage 2.)
				The whole of this Teesta valley road, which was formerly the high-way into the north of Sikkim, has now fallen into complete disrepair. The road is impassable for animals, and the cane bridges are mostly ricketty and rotten ; it is only used by foot passengers for local purposes, and has been entirely superseded by the new Gantok-Tumlong-Samatek road.

Route No. 12.

From GNATHONG to CHUMBI (*viâ* Jelep La).

Authority and date.—As in Route Book, and Captain F. C. Colomb, 42nd Gurkha Rifles, May and June 1895.

No. of stages.	Names of stages.	Distances.		Remarks.
		Inter-mediate.	Total.	
1	Kophu, or Kupup . .	5	5	Road leaves Gnathong and descends moraine slope for some 150 feet and then ascends in a north-easterly direction the hill slopes on the right bank of the Gnathong stream, reaching the Tuko La, elevation, 13,550 feet in 2 miles ; gradients 1 in 6, road a narrow rough stony track, hill-sides open and slopes generally easy. The Tuko La ridge faces north and is an excellent position from which to command the road to the Jelep La. Thence an easy descent and ascent of some 300 feet, road rounding the head of a gently sloping open valley to the Nim La ridge at 3 miles ; hence a steady descent over a rough road, but gradients easy, round the north of the flat valley in which lies the Bidang Tso (lake), a sheet of water about one mile long by ⅓ a mile wide. From its southern extremity a path leads to the Donchuk La formerly called the Pemberingo pass (*vide* Route 16). Cross a low ridge thickly covered with rhododendron scrub and a strip of marshy ground ; at 5 miles cross the Jelep stream, which is at all times fordable, by a log foot-bridge. Here the road up the Jelep turns off right. On the right bank of the Jelep stream is Kophu, a large open undulating

Route No. 12—contd.

No. of stages.	Names of stages.	Distances.		Remarks.
		Intermediate.	Total.	
				tract, marshy in places, on which 1,500 men could encamp; fuel, rhododendron scrub, plentiful in vicinity; elevation, 12,700 feet. Kophu is commanded by Tent hill, so called from its shape, which rises 1,000 feet with a very steep even slope from the edge of the camping-ground to the north-east. Hill-sides open and rocky.
2	YATUNG . . .	9½	14½	Path is up the right bank of the Jelep stream and is fairly level but wretchedly bad for ¾ mile when a short steep ascent leads to an open ridge within 1,500 yards of the summit of the pass. Hence the road is easy, the lower slopes of the hills over which it passes being gentle. The Jelep pass (elevation 14,390 feet) is a saddle some 400 yards long, at either end of which rise precipitous rocks, some 400 feet higher than the pass itself. Those to the north-west are less precipitous than those to the south-east, but in both cases they are accessible only to infantry. About 500 yards short of the summit on the Sikkim side there is a wide open space where 1,000 men could encamp, water from stream running down valley, rhododendron scrub for fuel would have to be brought from a mile down the pass. Country bare and rugged. During the winter the pass is closed by snow, which falls to a great depth. It is possible to reach the Donchuk La (Pemberingo pass) direct from the Jelep, but there is practically no path and very difficult country has to be crossed (vide Route No. 18). On the Tibet side of the Jelep La the hills open out enclosing a bare crater-like valley. The path is rough and stony and descends rapidly to a small lake called the Chola Tso, falling 600 feet in the first ½ of a mile, it then passes along the southern shore of the lake. This descent may be made more gradual by taking the military road which keeps to the hill-side to the north and descends more gently. Road now drops down a spur very steeply to the valley of the Langrang river, rough and stony. Here there is a camping-ground for 1,500 men called Byuthang. Enter fir and rhododendron jungle, road very bad, boggy and rocky, roughly following the left bank of the Langrang river. At about 3¼ miles pass Langrang, elevation 12,930 feet, where there is a stone rest-house built for European merchants but never used, and a fair camping-ground for a regiment if tents were crowded together. Path now leaves the main valley and drops down a spur through thick jungle due north crossing a fordable tributary stream by a rough plank bridge immediately beyond which there is a clearing called Tarchung, elevation 11,278 feet, where a regiment could encamp; thence along bank of stream to its junction with the main river, road rough and stony, many tributary streams being crossed, most of which are roughly bridged with logs. At Damkochen, a clearing, elevation 11,176 feet, is a stony camping-ground for 500 men, and almost immediately after passing this the first bridge over the Langrang river is reached. Path crosses the river six times in the last mile and a half by strong log bridges averaging 6 feet wide, without hand rails. The valley here is very narrow and thickly wooded and the road is bad, being rough and rocky and crossing numerous boggy hollows. Yatung is reached immediately after crossing the last bridge at the junction of the Nathu and Langrang streams; here the lower road from the Nathu La joins in. Yatung consists of the house of the Commissioner of Chinese Customs, four blocks of shops and a Tibetan guard-house; the whole form a rough square, are built of stone and wood and occupy a flat space some 50 yards broad between the hill-side and the river which is now called the Yatung Chu. The Nathu stream joins the main river immediately below the settlement of Yatung. The house of the Commissioner of Chinese Customs stands in the centre of a stone wall enclosure, 25 × 20 yards in area, the walls being 10 feet high and 2½ feet thick; there are no loopholes or arrangements for defence. The lower storey of the house is stone and the upper light wood-

Route No. 12—*contd.*

No. of stages.	Names of stages.	Distances.		Remarks.
		Inter-mediate.	Total.	
				work and lath and plaster. The western side of the outer wall is built against the hill-side, and at the south-west angle one can step off the hill-side on to the roof of the servants' houses. The main road passed between the shops and the Commissioner's house. The shops number 18 in four blocks, the outer walls being stone; the two larger blocks are each about 25 yards long and the smaller each about 18 yards. These shops, which were intended for traders, are unoccupied except by the Chinese customs officials. The Tibetan guard-house comprises two stone buildings in the north-west corner of the settlement; the most easterly of the two has a raised platform about the height of the top of the wall which could be used as a banquette, but the buildings, which are of stone, are not loopholed. The accommodation available at Yatung is roughly 20 men to each shop, 40 in the Tibetan guard-house and 50 in the Commissioner's enclosure. The position of Yatung is one incapable of defence against a well armed enemy as it is commanded east and west at ranges of 50 yards, the hills rising very steeply on either side to a considerable height; those to the east and south-west are wooded, those to the north-west open.
				A regiment could encamp on the river bank above and below Yatung and on a flat open spur to the north of and 100 feet immediately above the settlement. Fuel plentiful, but no supplies.
				From the top of the Jelep pass to Yatung is 7 miles and the road is regularly travelled by laden mules, but the gradients are in places as much as 1 in 6 and the road is in general bad, rocky, and boggy. Elevation of Yatung, 11,000 feet.
3	CHUMBI	5½	20	Leaving Yatung the road is level for 100 yards to the Nathu stream, which is crossed by a strong wooden bridge, stream is only a few yards wide but is some 3 feet deep and would be difficult to ford owing to the strength of the current.
				Just beyond the bridge a path turns off left up-hill to the Kajui monastery, distant about 1 mile. Valley now opens out, is free from forest and the road generally improves. Road keeps level and good along left bank of the Yatung river for 300 yards to the Chinese wall which is built right across the valley, occupying the whole of the flat portion (about 100 yards) and ascending the hill-slope for about the same distance on either side. It averages 15 feet in height and is 10 feet thick at the base. Along the summit are alternate embrasures and loopholes, the parapet here being about 2½ feet thick and built of stone, as is the whole wall. The mortar used is of inferior quality and the wall is one which would apparently be easily destroyed by artillery fire.* At either extremity are stone blockhouses, but the only flank defences are the north-west blockhouse and the gateway, the latter only affording flank fire for two or three rifles. The garrison is 20 Chinese and 8 Tibetans, who are unarmed. The wall is roofed over from end to end and the sections on either side of the stream are connected by a plank bridge. Access to the banquette is by means of stone steps at intervals along the rear of the wall. The wall may easily be outflanked by advancing over the open hill sides towards the Kajui monastery. The road to Chumbi passes through a gateway in the wall which can be closed by wooden doors which are not rifle-proof; and immediately in rear of the gate are rows of single-storied stone houses on either side of the road where the guard have their quarters. Close to the Kajui monastery is a small stone fort which commands the road below. At 1 mile from Yatung the road enters a forest of silver fir; gradients in this portion do not exceed 1 in 10. Just before entering Rinchengong is a sharp, short ascent of 200 yards followed by a rough descent which is in places very steep.

* This wall was destroyed by the earthquake in 1897 and again by floods in 1899. It was re-built by the Chinese on each occasion.

No. of stages.	Names of stages.	Distances.		Remarks.
		Inter-mediate.	Total.	
				Rinchengong is situated on the right bank of the Mo Chu and is bisected by the Jelep stream, which is spanned by a good bridge. The Mo Chu is also bridged a little below Rinchengong; this river is 50 yards wide and very rapid. Rinchengong contains 15 well-constructed houses, arranged in double stories, the lower being stone and the upper earth and plaster, roofs of planks. There are stretches of cultivation about the village on either bank of the Mo Chu. There is a path leading direct from Rinchengong to the Donchuk pass up a very steep spur. The Chumbi Valley is 300 to 600 yards wide in the vicinity of Rinchengong, and troops would have no difficulty in finding a camping-ground. Fuel plentiful.
				From Rinchengong Chumbi lies north-north-west up the right bank of the Mo Chu. Road is 6 feet wide and rises with an imperceptible gradient; it passes at times between stone walls, and at others over stretches of pasture land; hills on either side of the valley are steep and rocky, on the north-east slopes and lower spurs of the southern slopes are patches of silver fir forest. Elevation of the valley is about 9,300 feet. Galling (6 houses on the left bank of the Mo Chu) is passed at ⅔ mile. This village is the residence of all the Chief Tibetan officials of the lower Chumbi valley. At 1½ miles Phema village with 10 or 12 double-storied houses similar to those at Rinchengong, and here the path from the Nathu La joins the main road. The Mo Chu is spanned by a good cantilever bridge, 100 feet in length, just above Phema. A quarter of a mile beyond Phema is Pebithang, a new village containing about 70 houses inhabited solely by the Chinese officials of the Chumbi valley and their suite. About ¼ mile before reaching Chumbi the valley narrows to a width of 200 yards and the road passes over a steep, narrow ridge about 50 feet above the stream; this forms a strong defensive position. The road from Cho La is seen to the south-west descending a valley some 200 yards broad and crossing the small stream draining the valley by a rough plank bridge; this road joins the main road at Chumbi.
				Chumbi is situated on the right bank of the Mo Chu, and consists of the palace* and some ½ dozen other houses. Its position is such as to command all approaches by the Cho La, Nathu La, and Jelep La roads. The main road to Phari crosses from the right to the left bank of the Mo Chu at Chumbi by a good cantilever bridge 100 feet in length with an 8-foot roadway. There is a good camping-ground for a force of 2,000 men on the left bank of the Mo Chu at Chumbi with water from the river. Fuel from fir forest on neighbouring hill slopes. The people of the Chumbi valley are prosperous and the arable land of the valley is sufficient to support three times the present population. There is unlimited grazing for animals.
				The road from the Jelep La is on the whole bad, the gradients in places being as much as 1 in 6. There are no difficulties in the way of making a good bridle path.

* The palace is a large rambling three-storied building, round which the rest of the village is built.

Route No. 13.

From GNATHONG to CHUMBI (*via* Nathu La).

Authority and date.—Captain F. C. Colomb, 42nd Gurkha Rifles, 1895.

No. of stages.	Names of stages.	Distances.		Remarks.
		Inter-mediate.	Total.	
1	Yewkongteng	9	9	The Gnathong-Jelep-Chumbi road (*vide* Route No. 12) is followed as far as Kophu or Kupup, 5 miles.
				Path north-west keeping on the right bank of the Jelep stream which flows into the Menmo Tso gorge. Open grassy undulating country for one mile, path generally rough and stony. On reaching fir forest at the edge of the gorge the path turns north, crosses a small stream and winds round a spur, here it is narrow and dangerous to mules. It then descends 450 feet very steeply, gradients being as much as ¼, crosses the Meumo stream, which is always fordable, by rough log foot bridges, and ascends for an equal distance the opposite slope. The path across the gorge is exceedingly bad and can only be traversed by mules with great difficulty; it is rocky throughout and fir trees growing close to the path in places require felling. To the south-west of the road and about 1½ miles distant lies the Menmo Tso (lake), which is surrounded on all sides, except to the south-west, or exit end, by steep fir-clad hills. To the north-east the valley ends abruptly in a rugged basin of precipitous rocks. On leaving the fir and rhododendron forest in the valley the path emerges on open grass land and now ascends for ¼ mile more gently, crossing several boggy places. Cross a low hill, elevation 12,600 feet, on the summit of which is a catrleshed tenanted from July to September, and descend gently to the exit stream from the Onak Tso, a shallow reedy lake lying in a flat marshy valley 1½ by ½ mile. Cross the stream, which is always fordable, and leaving the lake to the right proceed up the valley for one mile by a very stony bad path, which, however, is almost level. The ground here is a mass of rivulets which drain the low, rhododendron-clad range to the west of the road. The valley is closed to the north-west by a moraine formation rising 150 feet above the general level; up this the path ascends easily and just below the summit are some almost flat, though somewhat marshy, stretches where half a regiment might encamp if scattered; the south-east slopes are open and grassy, those facing north-west thickly covered with rhododendron scrub. Water plentiful and good from numerous springs in the hill-side to the south-west of camp. Elevation, 13,150 feet.
				A path turns off here to the Lagyap La, by which Gantok may be reached. (*Vide* Route No. 14.)
2	Yatung	10¼	19½	Ascend the Yewkongteng spur north-east by a well marked path; for the first ½ mile the road is level; a small fordable stream is then crossed and an open spur ascended by an easy gradient. At 1 mile from camp the road from Gantok joins in from the west and hence the ascent is gentle to the pass. Two lakes are left to the right of the road and below it, and the valley gradually closes in as the Nathu La is approached. Reach the pass at 2 miles, elevation 14,250 feet, ascent from camp 1,100 feet. The pass is an open saddle, 100 yards long commanded on either side by rocky heights which terminate in inaccessible peaks; the slope immediately to the west of the pass may be scaled by infantry and the pass thus turned.
				Descend easily by a low open spur for 1½ miles to the Nathu or Chumdhe stream which is crossed to the left bank by a stone foot-bridge; stream fordable at all seasons. Here is an open, undulating maidan called Shang-la Thang, where a regiment could encamp.

Route No. 13—*contd.*

No. of stages.	Names of stages.	Distances.		Remarks.
		Inter-mediate.	Total.	
				At this spot the upper Nathu La road turns off left (north-west). Path now descends rather steeply 200 feet along the rocky bank of the stream, after which the valley for a bit is flat and the path good, but the scrub rhododendron is thick in places. At 4½ miles, at a spot called Champi Thang, elevation 12,950 feet, fir forest is entered and path descends gradually to an open flat where 400 men could encamp at 5½ miles. The valley now commences to close in and the rhododendron and fir forest is in places very thick. At 6½ miles is another fair camping-ground for 500 men called Chudung Thang, elevation 12,552 feet, and a little futher on yet another clearing of the same size called Chonama. At 9½ miles the path leaves the left bank of the stream which it has so far followed and winds round the head of a secondary valley descending very gradually over an open hill-side, and finally reaches Yatung just below the settlement.
3	CHUMBI . . .	5½	25	Hence to Chumbi, see Route No. 12.
				Alternative Route.
				The Upper Nathu La road.
2	CHUMBI . . .	12	21	The Upper Nathu La road leads direct to Phema, one mile south of Chumbi thus avoiding the defences at Yatung. It turns off the main route down the valley at Shang-la Thang 1½ miles from the summit of the pass on the Tibet side. The spot is easily recognised, as it is about 200 yards beyond the foot bridge and above the spot at which the stream makes a sudden descent of 200 feet in a series of cascades.
				The path rises very slightly at first along the slopes on the left bank of the stream and keeps along the open hill-sides; here it is rough and stony for a very short distance, but is not so bad as to prevent mules travelling along it. At 4½ miles from Yewkongteng (2⅔ from the Nathu La) is an open, flat spur over which flows a considerable stream; here 400 men could encamp if scattered; a steepish rocky climb through bush jungle ascending 150 feet follows, and then the path is fairly level for ¾ of a mile to a spur on which are some cattlesheds; here a regiment could encamp, water and pine fuel plentiful. At the cattleshed a path turns off north-east through pine forest; it is said to lead to the Kajui monastery. The main path now turns sharp to the left and ascends 250 feet passing through scrub jungle and emerging on gently sloping downs within 500 feet of the summit of the ridge.
				A few open grassy spurs are rounded, the path passing just below a saddle at 7 miles. For the next two miles path as before rounding gently sloping spurs with here and there scattered fir trees; hill slope rises about 250 feet above road to the left and is perfectly open. At 9 miles there is a cattleshed and here the road is along the summit on the ridge which a little distance on becomes clothed with fir forest and descends rapidly towards the Chumbi valley; elevaiton 13,700 feet; path now drops down spur apparently at an easy gradient forking some distance down, the right hand path leading to the Kajui monastery and the left directly into Phema. Distance to Phema from Yewkongteng about 11 miles.
				This path is passable throughout to mule carriage, but the jungle on either side of the road requires clearing and here and there rocks should be removed; at times the route passes through thick scrub jungle and patches of fir forest, but generally keeps just above the limit of trees. Beyond the first cattleshed mentioned the hill-

Route No. 13—*concld.*

No. of stages.	Names of stages.	Inter-mediate.	Total.	REMARKS
				side is seamed with paths which are greatly used by cattle and mules, these animals being driven up from the Chumbi valley to graze on the upper slopes. The two Nathu La routes on the Tibet side are infinitely preferable to the Jelep, though slightly longer from Gnathong. These paths are neither so rough nor so steep as that over the Jelep La, the camping-grounds are better and the jungle in the lower valleys is less dense. The Nathu La too, is some 140 feet lower than the Jelep La, and has always less snow on it. The objection to this route on the Sikkim side is that the Menmo Tso gorge has to be crossed from Gnathong; to obviate the difficulties in this gorge, however, very little road-making is necessary.

Route No. 14.

From GNATHONG to GANTOK (*vid* LAGYAP LA).

Authority and date.—REPORT ON CHUMBI VALLEY, 1895; AND POLITICAL OFFICER, SIKKIM, 1900.

No. of stages.	Names of stages.	Inter-mediate.	Total.	REMARKS.
1	YEWKONGTENG	9	9	For this road, see Route No. 13, stage 1.
2	LAGYAP LA	12	21	Leaving the moraine descend a gentle rhododendron-clad slope for 150 feet crossing a fordable stream flowing down from the Nathu La at ¼ mile, then along the gentle northern slopes of the Phenpsu valley which is flat, open and boggy, and some 500 yards long by 400 wide. At ¾ mile cross a second small stream and ascend northern slopes of valley over an open rock-studded slope for 100 yards striking the regular route from Gantok to the Nathu Ta at 1¼ miles from camp. The Phenpsu valley ends precipitously to the north-east, the stream plunging down a rocky fall into a deep fir-clad gorge; to the south-west of the valley the hills rise some 800 feet and are gently sloping and thickly clad with rhododendron, to the north-east they are higher and open but rocky and precipitous. After joining the main route the path for ¼ mile is rocky and leads along a precipitous hill-side with a valley 800 feet deep and thickly wooded with pine to the left. At 1½ mile pass a small flattish open space called Sharah, where a path turns off to the Yak La, north, after which descend 50 feet to the end of a lake 700 yards long by 200 yards wide crossing the exit stream which is always fordable; elevation 13,000 feet. Hence ascend 250 feet in ¾ of a mile by a rough, rocky path, in places crossing a series of stone steps and reach at 2¼ miles an open rolling plateau, 250 yards in diameter, also called Sharah, where a company could encamp if scattered, but the ground is rough and for the greater part of the year marshy. Cross a stream which drains a large lake lying further up the valley, by a series of stepping stones (elevation 13,250 feet) and turning south-west ascend for one mile to the summit of the Sebu La, elevation 13,600 feet, distance from camp 3¼ miles. This portion of the road is better, but is rocky in places, gradients not more than ⅓. The pass is a narrow opening between low rocks, the slopes

Route No. 14—*contd.*

No. of stages.	Names of stages.	Distances.		Remarks.
		Intermediate.	Total.	
				immediately to either flank rising some 50 feet higher; to the north the range rises gradually in masses of rock, till at the distance of a mile they reach an elevation of 14,400 feet.

Descend the head of the Tiphu valley abruptly, gradients as much as ½, by a steep, rough rocky path following the left bank of a small torrent; at one spot the track passes between two rocks through which only a very lightly laden mule can pass; the lower portion of the descent is over loose stones which roll away from under the feet. After ¼ of a mile of descent reach the upper extremity of the flat, open Tiphu valley, elevation 13,000 feet; the valley is enclosed on the east by steep rhododendron-clad hills, and on the west by bare slopes which, higher, give place to precipices and pinnacles of rock. At Tiphu there is ample camping accommodation for a regiment. Cross a small stream and in the next 1½ miles ascend 150 feet to the Lachung Karo La, reaching the summit, elevation 13,150 feet, at 5¼ miles; the path along this portion of the route is better and follows the gently sloping open hill-sides of the north-western end of the valley. The final ascent to the pass after passing a small lake called Sanketten is steepish for 100 feet, but can be traversed without difficulty by mules.

The Lachung Karo La is a narrow saddle, the slopes to either flank being thickly clothed with rhododendron scrub, but not rising more than 30 or 40 feet above the pass. Descend easily for ¼ mile, 150 feet, by a stony road to Chaungu, an open flat space some 400 yards across, overlooking the Tani Tso, elevation 13,000 feet; here there is camping space sufficient for a regiment. Hills on either side rise only two or three hundred feet above the valley, and are thickly covered with rhododendron scrub. Here a path turns off north over the Tani La, an open grassy saddle, 200 feet above Chaungu, to the Cho La (*vide* Route No. 15).

From Chaungu descend west over an open grassy slope ¾ of a mile to the Tani Tso, a lake about 1 mile long by ½ mile wide, shut in to the north and south by steep hills which incline sharply to the water's edge, elevation 12,450 feet. At the upper end of the lake 1,500 men might encamp in the dry season of the year, but at any other time the whole hillside is marshy and water-logged; rhododendron fuel in plenty. The path keeps to the north shore of and about 50 feet above the level of the lake, and is undulating stony, and difficult, in places passing over high steps from rock to rock. At the western end of the lake the path descends to the water's edge and strikes the right bank of the exit stream, the Tani Chu entering fir forest. The first descent is ½ for ¼ of a mile and is rough but after this it becomes gentle. At 2½ miles from the lake the Yali Chu is crossed close to its junction with the Tani Chu; so far from the Tani Tso the road has been throughout through fir forest without undergrowth, there being many open clearings in which a force of a couple of companies could camp; the final descent to the Yali Chu of 300 feet is steep, gradient ⅓; the river is an unfordable torrent 25 yards wide, bank low and thickly covered with bush jungle and fir forest. The river is crossed by a rough log cantilever bridge 26 yards long in all, the central span being 7 yards, roadway 6 feet wide and 10 feet above the stream, no hand rails; elevation 10,850 feet.

Path now follows right bank of the Yali Chu for 2 miles to camp and is very rough and rocky through thick fir and bush jungle, crossing numerous small streams and finally leaving the stream and turning to the right up an open marshy side valley which leads, after an ascent of 50 feet, to small marsh and a saddle on the main range where a company would find a

Route No. 14—*concld.*

No. of stages.	Names of stages.	DISTANCES.		REMARKS.
		Intermediate.	Total.	
				difficulty in encamping, though there is no lack of level ground in among the rhododendron trees on the saddle and numerous overhanging rocks under which a small force could bivouack. Water from the Yali Chu ¼ mile distant as the supply on the spot is bad. Fuel in plenty. Elevation 10,250 feet. There is a small 2-roomed wooden bungalow; stone chimneys; iron roof. There are also wooden lines to accommodate 10 mules or ponies.
				The above is an exceedingly hard march for either mules or coolies, and unless the transport is very lightly laden the march should be broken by halting at Chaungu.
3	GANTOK . . .	13	34	From the bungalow the road runs level for ¾ mile skirting the hill-side in a southerly direction. Hence the road gradually descends to Gantok, winding round the hill-side. The trace is a good one, the ascents and descents being gentle, average gradient $\frac{1}{15}$. For the first few miles the road runs through pine and rhododendron forest, and afterwards through thick bamboo jungle, emerging close to the Intchi monastery. There are two coolie rest-camps on the road at the 3rd and 8th miles from Lagyap. Water plentiful all along the road. This is the new road and has only recently been completed; it requires constant repairs, and some work would generally be necessary on it before laden animals could pass.
				The old road to Lagyap passes below the new road on leaving Gantok and goes down steeply to the bed of the Roro Chu; hence rising at a steep gradient to Lagyap—a long, tiring ascent. This road is very bad and has fallen into disuse.
				For Gantok, see Route 4.

Route No. 15.

FROM GNATHONG TO CHOLA.

Authority and date.—CAPTAIN F. C. COLOMB, 42ND GURKHA RIFLES, JULY AND SEPTEMBER 1895.

No. of stages.	Names of stages.	DISTANCES.		REMARKS.
		Intermediate.	Total.	
1	YEWKONGTENG . .	9	9	*Vide* Routes Nos. 12 and 13.
2	CHAUNGU . . .	5¾	14¾	Follow Route No. 14 as far as Chaungu.
3	CHOMNAGO . . .	7¾	22½	From Chaungu turn north and ascend for ½ a mile to the Tani La, a broad open grassy saddle, to which the ascent is very gentle; elevation 13,300 feet. Hence a very bad rocky descent over boulders and jagged rocks through dense rhododendron jungle for ¾ mile to the Yali Chu; the descent is only practicable to coolies and the most lightly laden mules. The Yali Chu, a stream flowing here in a gravelly bed, is 15 yards wide, 1½ feet deep; at other spots it is narrower and deeper. The valley is flattish and grassy averaging 100 yards wide; elevation 12,600 feet. Just across the stream is a flat open space where a regiment could encamp, called Byuthang, while above and below are other open tracts of equal extent. The hills rise from 600 to 1,000 feet on either side, are open to the

Route No. 15—*contd.*

No. of tages.	Names of stages.	Distances. Intermediate.	Distances. Total.	Remarks.
				north and densely clad with rhododendron to be south. There are cattle encampments in the Yali Chu valley in July to September whence about 10 coolies are obtainable. The Yali Chu valley is shut in to the north-east by precipitons rocky hills rising 1,500 feet above the valley. About ¼ mile above where the stream is crossed a path turns off right up the hill-side leading to the Yak La, *viâ* the Yethang La. From Byuthang the path for the first ¼ mile ascends the right bank of the Yali Chu rising gently over open ground; it then turns north up the hill-side which is open but very rocky in places. At ¾ mile, elevation 13,150 feet, pass to the right of a small lake lying in a hollow on the hill-side. The ascent continues for 1½ miles (2¾ from Chaungu) by fairly good path to the summit of the Byusa La, the last 500 yards being over undulating ground studded with enormous blocks of rock. A hundred yards short of the summit the path passes between two perpendicular rocks, 25 feet high; that on the right is surmounted by the remains of a stone hut formerly tenanted by a Lama, while on the left is a small outcrop of limestone used as a shrine. The Byusa La is an open saddle 100 yards long overlooking, towards the north, a small, bare undulating valley called Byusathang. Elevation of pass 13,650 feet; hill slopes on either side of the saddle gentle and open. Descent commences by crossing Byusathang, elevation 13,500 feet, then ¼ mile from pass (3 from Chaungu), turn north-west down the bank of the stream draining the valley leaving two lakes called Gainsala Tso or Byuksa Tso below the road to the left; for a short distance the road is fairly level along an open, gently sloping hill-side, it then turns north into a narrow, shallow valley and is very rocky and bad up to 4½ miles: here a small marsh is crossed and dense fir and rhododendron jungle entered. Path now plunges suddenly down a steep spur, the gradients in places being as much as ⅓. This descent continues to the Dik Chu at 5½ miles, and after rain becomes impassable to laden mules as it gets muddy and slippery. The Dik Chu is a rapid torrent, 25 yards wide and 2½ feet deep, which becomes unfordable after heavy rain; ample material is at hand all along the valley for bridge building; heavy rhododendron and other jungle along the left bank of the stream, the right is more open. The river is crossed at a spot called Begirup, no village; elevation 12,300 feet. Path now turns up the right bank and rises gently through bush jungle. At 6¼ miles cross the stream which drains the Tambia Tso by a rough foot bridge of three logs; stream fordable; 200 yards on cross a second small stream. At 7¼ miles a stone cattleshed in ruins, and here a path turns up the hill left to the Tambia Tso. A quarter of a mile on cross the Chomnago Chu, a fordable stream, by a rough foot bridge and reach Chomnago, a small grassy flat at the junction of the Chomnago Chu and the stream from the Cho La. The spot is marshy and would not afford space for more than six small tents, but there are large overhanging rocks about the camp under which 50 men could bivouack. Fuel, rhododendron and fir in plenty. Elevation, 12,600 feet. A precipice 800 feet high overhangs Chomnago to the north. Road passable to lightly laden mules in fine weather when the descent to the Dik Chu is not impracticable.
4	Cho La . . .	4¼	26¾	Ascend east up the right bank of the Dik Chu, which flows down from the Cho La for ⅓ of a mile by a good path through bush jungle to a small open grassy space where two companies could encamp; elevation

No. of stages.	Names of stages.	DISTANCES.		REMARKS.
		Intermediate.	Total.	
				12,875 feet; here a path turns off almost due north and ascends the hill-side into the valley of the Chomnago Chu, crossing that stream and again ascending over the precipice which overhangs Chomnago, and finally descends into the valley of the Tambia Tso; this path is very narrow and little used and is passable only to coolies. Its starting point is difficult to find and for the first ½ mile it is much obstructed by bush jungle.
				The main path up the valley leaves the Dik Chu here to avoid the moraines of large boulders which line the banks, and turning north zig-zags up the hill-side through rhododendron and bush jungle. At 1¼ miles the hill-side becomes more open and the path turns east following the contour of the hill and rising 400 feet in the next mile.
				At 2¾ miles reach a flat valley, elevation 14,000 feet, country quite open, hills rising about 1,000 feet above the valley, the slopes facing north being covered with thin rhododendron jungle, while those facing south are open, grassy, and rocky. Here the path strikes the right bank of the Dik Chu again which at this elevation is a mere brook.
				Leaving a small lake, called the Patheng Tso, to the right the path is now level along the right bank of the stream for ½ a mile; an easy but rough and rocky ascent for ¾ of a mile following. Another flat, bare, rocky valley, elevation 14,600 feet, is now reached; here there is a second small lake to the south of which rise two bare, inaccessible, rocky peaks, their summits being some 800 feet above the valley. To the north the hills are lower, open and accessible to infantry.
				Leaving the small lake to the right the path now ascends 50 feet in the next ¼ mile to the summit of the Cho La, elevation 14,550 feet. Total ascent from Chomnago 2,000 feet in 4¼ miles.
				The pass is a long open saddle which it would be difficult to defend with a force of less than 1,000 men as it is easily outflanked from either side. To the right and left of the pass bare, open, rocky slopes rise very gently in terraces from 5 to 30 feet in height; to the south is a long flat saddle some 300 feet higher than the pass, and by crossing which the Yak La may be reached in an hour as compared with a long day's march if moving on the Sikkim side of the frontier (*vide* Route No. 19).
				A brigade could encamp at the pass if scattered: water plentiful but no fuel.
				The earlier portion of this stage as far as the Patheng Tso shows signs of having at one time been kept carefully in repair. The trace is good, it having originally been a cut bridle-path some 3 feet wide. This portion is passable to mules throughout.
				The upper half is not in such good order, there being many slippery, sloping slabs of rock over which mules would have a difficulty in climbing. On the whole, lightly laden mules accustomed to travelling in rough country might be taken to the summit of the pass though not beyond.
				The Cho La is not defended by stone walls as is the case with the passes further south.
				From Cho La to Chumbi.
				The Cho La route leads directly into Chumbi, the distance from the summit of the pass being said to be 9 miles.

Route No. 15—*concld.*

No. of stages.	Names of stages.	Distances.		Remarks.
		Inter-mediate.	Total.	
				On leaving the summit of the pass a small flat valley is traversed for a few hundred yards; then descend slightly to a very narrow valley choked with huge boulders and shut in by precipices to either flank. The valley now makes a sudden bend to the north and the path descends along the edge of the stream which falls in a series of cascades, some of which are 30 feet high. Down the sides of these waterfalls the path leads in rough stone steps. The valley again turns east and opens out, the path crossing the stream twice over rough and rocky ground. Beyond this there is no further difficulty, the left bank of the stream being followed down a flat open valley; hill-slopes to the north open, those to the south covered with dense scrub rhododendron. The stream is fordable anywhere. At 4 miles are the Rabdo Tso lakes where a regiment might encamp if scattered. (Personal inspection of route ceased here.) At the lakes the path ascends the face of the northern hill-slopes and finally as the range decreases in elevation runs along the summit of the ridge, eventually dropping into Chumbi. Viewed from the hill-top above the Kajui monastery the road appears level and in good order up to the point where the descent commences. The route from the summit of the Cho La is in its present condition passable only to cooly transport.

Route No. 16.

From GNATHONG to DONCHUK LA (PEMBERINGO PASS) and DOKA LA.

Authority and date.—Captain F. C. Colomb, 42nd Gurkha Rifles, May 1895.

No. of stages.	Names of stages.	Distances.		Remarks.
		Inter-mediate.	Total.	
1	Kophu or Kupup	5	5	*Vide* Route No. 12.
2	Donchukthang	4	9	Turn back along the Gnathong road for a few hundred yards then strike off south-east to the northern end of the Bidang Tso (lake); path is then at times along the water's edge and at others 50 feet above its surface over stony and marshy ground. At the south-east extremity of the lake turn north-east up a narrow gorge, path being up the right bank of the stream; it is rough and rocky in places, but is passable to local transport animals. The ascent up the valley is gentle and the valley gradually opens out and becomes flatter. Camp on a flat but marshy tract at the junction of two streams below the point at which the path ascends a spur to the Donchuk La. Space for three regiments to encamp, if scattered, water good from the stream; rhododendron and fir fuel plentiful ½ a mile down the valley. Elevation 13,130 feet. The camp is commanded on all sides by open hills which rise from 1,000 to 2,000 feet above the valley. *Route from Donchuthang to Donchuk La (or Pemberingo Pass).* Distance 2 miles. Cross the stream at camp by a ford and then ascend the bare hill-side to the north-east. At first the ascent is very gentle, then the path zig-zags up a steep slope reaching an elevation of 13,830 feet ½ a mile from

No. of stages.	Names of stages.	DISTANCES.		REMARKS.
		Inter-mediate.	Total.	

camp. Hence for $1\frac{1}{2}$ miles over open, undulating ground to the Donchuk La, a bare ridge 200 yards long, commanded on both sides by rocky heights which are scaleable by infantry. These rocks rise 800 feet above the pass to the north and 500 feet to the south. Elevation of pass 14,300 feet. There are ruins of Tibetan walls at the summit and at intervals on the Sikkim side of the frontier. The descent from the pass towards Chumbi is easy for 500 feet, after which it runs along the level bed of a stream for 1 mile and then turns east down the valley.

Alternative passes.

There are two passes, 1,200 yards to the north, by which the Donchuk La may be turned. The path to these passes, which are the same elevation as the Donchuk La, leads up the valley to the west of the direct road and is easy for 1 mile ; here three lakes are passed after which there is a steep ascent over piled heaps of rock to the passes. This route is traversable only by infantry.

| 3 | LABATHANG | 7 | 16 | A very circuitous road necessitated by the intervention of a high rocky range running south-west. Cross the stream to the east of camp and ascend slightly through patches of rhododendron scrub crossing a second stream at $\frac{1}{4}$ mile. Here the path turns due south and ascends a gently sloping hill-side. At $\frac{3}{4}$ of a mile a good camp for 500 men on the shore of a small lake. At $1\frac{1}{2}$ miles reach a saddle just before which the path crosses boulders for 300 yards ; here the path is only passable to coolies. Up to this point the path is so badly marked as to be difficult to follow. Path now better marked for $\frac{3}{4}$ of a mile to a saddle where it turns north-east and descends rapidly over rough ground, then north-east by east keeping fairly level over marshy ground studded with rocks. Hence to camp there is no trace of a path owing to the route being so little used. Down the bed of a stream for 100 yards to a small narrow valley which is crossed and the opposite hill-side ascended to 14,700 feet elevation ; the ascent is steep and rocky. Descend 800 feet to the shore of a small lake ; here there is camping space for one company. Hence the general direction is south-east first rounding the northern slope of a knoll immediately above the lake, then crossing a rough, rocky, but fairly level spur dropping 150 feet to an open valley called Labathang where there is almost level ground on which two regiments could encamp. Good water and fuel (rhododendron scrub) in abundance. Elevation, 13,780 feet. |

Labathang to Naodonten La.

Distance 2 miles.

The path leads due north rising gently up the Labathang valley, then turns west up a bare hill-side ; here the path is very steep but good ; finally turning north again reach the pass, a rocky saddle on the summit of which is a small lake, elevation 14,800 feet. By this pass the route from the Donchuk La into Chumbi may be joined. Eight hundred feet below the pass on the Tibet side is a broad open valley studded with lakes ; here a brigade could encamp.

General direction, south.

| | DOKA LA . . | 5 | 21 | From Labathang descend suddenly keeping to the hill-side on the right bank of the stream, dropping 800 feet in $\frac{3}{4}$ of a mile, path well marked and passing through rhododendron scrub in a series of sharp zig-zags. At bottom of valley is a lake $\frac{1}{2}$ a mile long and 200 yards wide shut in to the east by high cliffs and masses of rock débris. Round the eastern end of the lake over masses of jagged rock then follow the |

Route No. 16—*concld.*

No. of stages.	Names of stages.	Inter-mediate.	Total.	Remarks.
				south-east shore to a point where a stream flows in. Turn up the stream and ascend about 2,000 feet in two miles, generally over rough ground; in places there are steep rocky bits over which no baggage animal could travel. After crossing the ridge the path keeps to the Tibetan face of the watershed and crosses, at first, rough ground which gradually gives place to the open rolling downs of the Doka La as the path descends. On these downs (elevation about 13,100 feet) a brigade could manœuvre and 5,000 men encamp. On the Tibetan side is a broad open valley only a few feet lower than the pass, through which flows a considerable stream sufficient for the requirements of 5,000 men; rhododendron and fir fuel plentiful at a distance of ½ a mile from the Doka La downs.

Route No. 17.

From GNATHONG to YAK LA.

Authority and date.—CAPTAIN F. C. COLOMB, 42ND GURKHA RIFLES, JUNE 1895.

No. of stages.	Names of stages.	Inter-mediate.	Total.	Remarks.
1	YEWKONGTENG	9	9	*Vide* Routes Nos. 12 and 13.
2	CAMP BELOW YAK LA ON THE CHUMBI SIDE.	6¾	15¾	For 1½ miles as far as Sharah follow the Gantok road, *vide* Route No. 14. Sharah is a small fairly level rock-strewn space just above a small lake.
				Here the route to the Yak La, a scarcely distinguishable path, turns off north and descends 100 feet by a gently sloping rock-strewn spur. It then crosses the eastern marshy shore of the lake, elevation 13,150 feet, and at 2½ miles ascends a gently sloping valley strewn with rocks and more thickly vegetated than is usual at this elevation. Turn west and ascend to a low saddle overlooking a second lake lying west of and 100 feet below the road; thence ascend gradually along an open spur, keeping along the eastern side of the valley to a lake 100 yards wide situated in a crater-like hollow at an elevation of 14,000 feet; distance 4½ miles. Here a company could encamp; rhododendron fuel in plenty just below the lake. The above is a very little used path and is very difficult to follow.
				The main path from Gantok to the Yak La (*vide* Route No. 21) passes to the north-west of and 200 feet above the lake; whichever side of the lake is taken the scramble up to this path is rough and difficult, the hill-side being strewn with huge rocks.
				Hence the main path rises gently but is very bad, here and there ascending in steps and at times passing over slippery sloping slabs of rock.
				Pass another small lake leaving it to the east and emerge at 5½ miles on a bare, flattish valley 100 yards wide and strewn with boulders; proceed up this valley for ½ a mile over nearly flat ground passing a small lake a few feet below the summit of the pass. Fifty men could encamp on the shore of the lake, but no fuel is available nearer than 1½ miles.
				The pass is a flattish saddle some 300 yards long, the slope to which on either side is very gentle. Elevation, 14,500 feet. There are no defences along the

Route No. 17—*concld.*

No. of stages.	Names of stages.	Distances.		Remarks.
		Inter-mediate.	Total.	
				summit; on either side of the pass rise rocky precipitous hills for 1,000 feet which might with difficulty be scaled by infantry.

After leaving the pass the path down into Chumbi is fairly level for ¾ of a mile keeping to the eastern slope of a low rocky spur. A quarter of a mile from the pass is a lake some 400 yards long about 150 feet above and along the western side of which the road passes. At the outlet from the lake a path turns off right and keeps to the northern slopes of the range; it is very badly marked and was found by natives who examined it to come to an end about 4 miles down the valley. At the lake outlet the main path turns north and descends slightly to an open, grassy valley, with an amphitheatre of precipices 300 yards to the west, over which falls a fine cascade, 200 feet high. Here a regiment could encamp; rhododendron fuel and water in plenty.

Between the Yak La and Camp the path is exceedingly bad, crossing as it does heaped up boulder and sloping sheets of a rock over which no laden baggage animal could pass. The same may be said of the route on the Sikkim side of the frontier.

Beyond the camping-ground the path turns east, becomes better and descends to the bottom of the valley, striking the Mo Chu at Phema.

Alternative route.

Along portions of this route there are signs of a path, but it is evidently very little used. It is not passable to animal carriage.

Starting from Yewkongteng (stage 2), ascend first by the path to the Nathu La, then on reaching the point at which the road from Gantok joins in turn off road and ascend hill-side north-east by an ill-marked path. The climb from Yewkongteng is 500 feet. Path now descends 200 feet and crosses a small stream, at the point at which it leaves a flattish stony valley backed to the right by an amphitheatre of precipitous cliffs. Thence ascend 300 feet almost due west up an easy slope by a badly marked path over slabs of rock and through rhododendron scrub reaching a saddle 13,900 feet in elevation immediately below the precipitous slopes of the main range. Here all traces of the path are lost. Turn north and keep along a sort of shelf with a sheer precipice to the left and a precipitous hill slope to the right; for a mile the ground is fairly level but very rocky, then a lake 200 yards long, elevation 14,000 feet, is reached; pass round its eastern shore and ascend the opposite open, gently sloping ridge to 14,150 feet, after which cross fairly level ground for ½ mile to a saddle, elevation 14,200 feet, whence ascend by a steep but unobstructed path up an open hillside to the crater-like valley and lake mentioned in the former route. Distance 4½ miles. Hence follow former route over the Yak La.

This alternative route lies throughout on the hill-slopes immediately above the direct route.

Route No. 18.

From DONCHUKTHANG (below DONCHUK LA) to JELEP LA.

Authority and date.—Captain F. C. Colomb, 42nd Gurkha Rifles, May 1895.

No. of stages.	Names of stages.	DISTANCES.		Remarks.
		Inter-mediate.	Total.	
1	Jelep La . . .	4	4	The route to the alternative passes to the Donchuk La is first followed; it leads up the valley north-north-east from Donchukthang, ascending about 1,000 feet to the three lakes (*vide* Route No. 16); hills at first open, then covered with rhododendron scrub; at the lakes all vegetation, except grass, ceases. Path very badly marked and difficult to follow. Pass between the first two lakes and ascend a spur which runs north-west and south-east and terminates west of the third or upper lake. Ascend over perfectly open ground by an easy slope for 600 feet to a saddle, then descend a steep rocky slope west. Cross a flat valley through rhododendron scrub and over rocks and pass between two lakes crossing a fordable rocky stream. Ascend open hill-side, due north, by fairly easy slope rising 800 feet to the Jelep Pass. Route is only passable to lightly laden coolies, and that with the greatest difficulty.

Route No. 19.

From YAK LA to RABDO TSO (below CHO LA on the CHUMBI side).

Authority and date.—Captain F. C. Colomb, 42nd Gurkha Rifles, June 1895.

No. of stages.	Names of stages.	DISTANCES.		Remarks.
		Inter-mediate.	Total.	
1	Rabdo Tso . . .	5	5	There is no path between the Yak La and the Rabdo Tso, but the country is so open as far as the summit of the range separating the Cho La and Yak La valleys in Chumbi that a force of infantry might easily turn the Cho La by a direct advance from the Yak La. The only difficulty encountered is the descent to the lake which is through thick rhododendron scrub. Leaving the Yak La descend by the Phema road (*vide* Route No. 13) for 300 yards and then turn north on to an open, uneven tableland keeping immediately below a series of small precipices which rise to the left. Pass two small tarns and continuing over open undulating ground, strike the southern or outlet end of a semi-circular lake, a mile long. Keep to the eastern shore of the lake for 1 mile, country as before and then ascend a rocky hill-side north-east. The ascent is steep and rocky but would form no obstacle to infantry as the ground is quite open. The summit of the range is a tableland 15,400 feet in elevation, consisting of a confused mass of straight layers of rock from 10 to 40 feet thick, forming precipices below which are many small pools of water. The Rabdo Tso is visible 2,000 feet below the summit. The descent is difficult being at first over precipitous rocks then through breast-high rhododendron and finally down the bed of a stream. The lakes are small pools where the river has widened, elevation 13,400 feet; a regiment could encamp here if scattered; fuel in plenty. The Cho La stream is easily fordable. The slopes of the valley which face south are open and grassy, those facing north are covered with very thick rhododendron scrub. This is a characteristic

Route No. 19—*concld.*

No. of stages.	Names of stages.	DISTANCES.		REMARKS.
		Inter-mediate.	Total.	
				common to all the higher valleys of Sikkim and the Chumbi valley.
				The Cho La may be reached direct from the Yak La in about 2 miles by keeping to the west shore of the semi-circular lake and ascending about 800 feet to a long flat saddle whence a short descent over rocky ground to the Cho La. Open country throughout easily traversable by infantry.

Route No. 20.

From GANTOK to CHO LA.

Authority and date.—SURGEON-CAPTAIN F. EWENS, I.M.S., 1895.

No. of stages.	Names of stages.	DISTANCES.		REMARKS.
		Inter-mediate.	Total.	
1	RUNKPO . . .	11½	11½	*General direction, north-east.* Leaving Gantok follow route No. 4 as far as the Penlong La, a good bridle-path in excellent order. Here the Runkpo path turns off the main road right and goes straight down hill following the bed of a watercourse for 3½ miles to the Dik Chu passing the village of Satak (or Cherta). Above and to the east of Cherta are some open slopes suitable for camping-grounds. At Cherta a path turns off left to Phensong, the path under report passing to the east of the village and crossing a small marsh after which it is down the right bank of a small ravine to the Dik Chu and is very steep and quite impracticable to any form of transport except coolies. The Dik Chu is crossed by a cane bridge, 50 feet long; altitude 3,950 feet. The river is unfordable at all seasons of the year. The construction of a permanent bridge would be a matter of no difficulty, as the banks of the river are high and timber is available on the spot. Path now ascends very steeply for 1¼ miles to the village of Lingcham, elevation 5,300 feet, through thick jungle with cultivation clearings here and there. Below Lingcham is a succession of small open plateaux which would form good camps; water and fuel on the spot. Thence to Runkpo, 1 mile, elevation 5,950 feet. Runkpo contains one house, and is situated on the Fieungong ridge, up which the Cho La road from Gantok and Tumlong runs; the two roads unite at Satha La. Water-supply limited; a small spring near village only flows in the rains; a second spring which would only supply a small detachment, half a mile down south slope of hill. From Penlong La the path is steep and stony and only passable to cooly transport.
2	DEMLACHEN . . .	7½	19	Ascend steeply up the ridge, following the crest of the Fieungong spur for 3 miles, path through bamboo jungle and passable to mule transport, in fair order but very narrow. No water and no camping-grounds available without clearing. At 3 miles an open grazing-ground on summit of ridge where two companies could encamp; scanty supply of water in pools; fodder abundant and bamboo hutting material available. At 5½ miles another open space; altitude 9,200 feet. Hence a very steep ascent passing at 6 miles. altitude 9,600 feet, a small spring and at 6½ a small cave on the left of the road where 20 men could bivouack; this cave is regularly used by natives passing up and down as a halting-place; no water. Hence ascend a steep rocky slope which is, however, passable to mules and at 7½ miles reach a ruined stone hut known as Demlachen, altitude 10,700 feet; no water.

Route No. 20—*concld.*

No. of stages.	Names of stages.	Distances.		Remarks.
		Intermediate.	Total.	
3	Cho La . . .	16½	35½	Ascend to the summit of Fienngong, 12,130 feet, distance 1¼ miles, passing a large open space which would afford a camping-ground for 1,000 men; water probably available as it is used as a cattle station. Rhododendron jungle is entered and the road becomes wider, less steep and the country more open. Path now keeps along the ridge which is pretty level or undulating for about a mile, a series of open slopes and several ruins of large stone houses being passed. A mile of steep ascent follows, two small caves being passed. Here another open space, ¼ mile long, is passed. Road is now much more open, then descends abruptly down a stony zig-zag for 1½ miles to a small open space called Bekup, altitude 11,600 feet. Water plentiful; camping-space for 100 men if ground were levelled for tents. Descending very steeply from Bekup, the Dik Chu is reached at 1 mile on at a place called Talong (11,000 feet); descent is almost too steep for mules. Hence the road rises gradually keeping to the right bank of the stream through fir forest. Two miles on is an open space called Barfonchen, where two regiments could encamp. Numerous small caves and some yak huts are passed. Pass Dumgo Chen, a large cave capable of sheltering 20 men, where there is a rude gateway of pine logs and a rock with a Tibetan inscription, elevation 12,100 feet, and a mile on reach Begirup, a grazing-ground, where the road over the Byusa La joins in. Hence it is 2 miles to Chomnago, and from there 4¼ to the Cho La (*vide* Route No. 15). *Note.*—This is on the whole a fair road, and in former days was regularly used by mules and ponies.

Route No. 21.

From GANTOK to YAK LA.

Authority and date.—Captain F. C. Colomb, 42nd Gurkha Rifles, September 1895.

No. of stages.	Names of stages.	Distances.		Remarks.
		Intermediate.	Total.	
1	Lagyap La . . .	15	15	For this march, see Route No. 14.
2	Byuthang . . .	7	22	Follow the Gnathong road (*vide* Route No. 14) to within ½ a mile of the Yali Chu bridge turning off to the left and passing the bridge about 200 feet higher up the hill-side. The hill-side above and to the west of the bridge is called Seramarbo. Half a mile beyond the bridge the valley opens out and a clearing and cattle station called Rolep is passed, elevation 11,000 feet; here a regiment could encamp. Three miles from Lagyap La a rocky torrent is crossed by a foot bridge of three logs, 10 yards long, stream unfordable after heavy rain. Two hundred yards beyond the stream a path turns off left and ascends the hill crossing the range to the west of the Byusa La and joining the road to Chomnago. The main path keeps level along the hill-side passing at 3¼ miles another flat open marshy space called Yahbirum where two companies could encamp. The road is then along the bank of the Yali Chu passing through a grassy valley 360 yards wide and ¾ mile long called Pamu-

Route No. 21—*concld.*

No. of stages.	Names of stages.	DISTANCES.		REMARKS.
		Inter-mediate.	Total.	
				thang; at the upper end of this open space is a slight ascent to a cattle station called Tikhu, elevation 11,700 feet. Here a patch of fir forest, ¼ mile wide, is passed through beyond which is a large gently sloping open space where two regiments could encamp, called Yumtho; elevation 12,000 feet. Beyond this point fir forest practically ceases and the valley is open and grassy, the hill slopes to the right of the road being densely clothed with scrub rhododendron. A rather rough climb for ½ mile over stony ground follows to Shingou, a flat valley, elevation 12,325 feet, and hence it is ½ a mile over open grass land to Byuthang (*vide* Route No. 15).
				The first half of this stage is not practicable to animal transport. The earlier portion of the stage is through dense rhododendron and fir forest.
				An alternative to this stage is to follow the Gnathong road as far as Chaungu above the Tani Tso and then cross the Tani La (*vide* Route No. 15). Though this route is perhaps easier as far as Chaungu, the objection to it is the very rocky descent from the Tani La to Byuthang, which is only passable to transport animals with great difficulty.
3	YAK LA · · · ·	8	30	From Byuthang the Yali Chu Valley takes a sharp turn to the north; the road ascends the gorge for 1½ miles to a small lake named Pyamokom Tso, elevation 13,600 feet, thence it keeps along a ridge for another mile to a tarn called Langbu Tso, elevation 14,000 feet; half a mile on the last lake is reached called Yagahchum Tso, elevation 14,300 feet, and ¾ mile further the summit of the Yethang La, 14,500 feet; the pass is a level sheet of bare rock 100 yards wide dividing the head-waters of the Yali and Rong Chus. Thence a slight descent for ¾ mile skirting a high precipitous ridge and later crossing the valley; this portion is bad and unrideable, passing chiefly over ancient moraine formations; five small lakes are passed, hill-sides bare and rugged. Here join Route No. 17 which is followed to the Yak La. At the summit of the Yak La (14,450 feet?) is the usual heap of stones and a remarkable rocking stone of some 12 tons in weight.
				The Yak La may be reached from Gantok, *viâ* Runkpo and Fieungong by crossing the Dik Chu where the river is struck at Begirup, 1½ miles short of Chomnago, and ascending to the Byusa La then dropping into the Yali Chu Valley at Byuthang (*vide* Routes Nos. 20 and 17).
				The Yak La is out of consideration as a route as it is a very difficult pass, the Nathu La, to which it is quite close, being a much easier road.

Route No. 22.

FROM GANTOK TO GIAOGONG.

Authority and date.—BRIGADIER-GENERAL A. G. YEATMAN-BIGGS, C.B., AUGUST 1896, AND CAPTAIN W. F. O'CONNOR, R. G. A., AUGUST 1900.

No. of stages.	Names of stages.	DISTANCES.		REMARKS.
		Inter-mediate.	Total.	
1	TUMLONG (6,550 feet) ·	13	13	After leaving Gantok (Residency, 6,000 feet) the road ascends gently to the Penlong La, 4½ miles (6,250 feet). It then descends (at 4½ miles, good stage for transport) to the Dik Chu bridge, 9 miles (2,700 feet), with a ruling gradient of 1/7, though it is steeper in places.

Route No. 22—*contd.*

No. of stages.	Names of stages.	Distances.		Remarks.
		Intermediate.	Total.	
				As far as this the road is generally 6 feet wide, sometimes narrower. The Dik Chu bridge is a simple iron suspension bridge, 92 feet span, 4' 6" wide in the clear, and well above the water. Owing to want of ties it is shaky when transport animals are passing over. Bad loads must be taken off owing to narrowness. Dik Chu unfordable here. There is level space for camping close by. Here changing place for mules. The road now ascends in zig-zags, very steeply, often ¼. It is rocky and narrow (4 feet in places). At 11½ miles it becomes less steep. At 12½ miles Phodong monastery. At 13 miles rest-house just above Labrong monastery. The whole road requires repairs and widening in places. A Pioneer regiment would put it right in a day. Water plentiful throughout. Just below Labrong is Tumlong, with the Raja's palace. Round Labrong there is camping ground for 400 or 500 men. Within a radius of ¼ mile 500 men could be sheltered in existing buildings. Water good and plentiful. Much bamboo forage within ¼ mile. The rest-house has three rooms, bathrooms, verandah, and outhouses.
				Branch Roads.
				Satha La, on the Fieungong ridge, is reached as follows :—
				I.—From Penlong La by steep footpath *viâ* Satak down to the Dik Chu crossed by cane or temporary bridge (not suitable for mules), then steep ascent (*vide* Route 20).
				II.—From Dik Chu bridge a mule path leads up left bank. Dik Chu has to be forded just above junction with Bokeha Chu, thence steep ascent to Satha La.
				III.—From Tumlong a mule path descends by zig-zags to Bokeha Chu, no mule bridge, then up to Satha La.
				From Satha La a road leads to the Cho La, see Route 20.
				From Dik Chu bridge a footpath, not good enough for mules, leads down left bank of Dik Chu to the Teesta at Samdong, where there is a cane bridge. It is too rapid here to swim mules across the Teesta.
				From Tumlong two roads lead down to the Teesta at Ringon,—one *viâ* Mafi La, and one *viâ* Detong monastery.
2	Samatek (6,961 feet)	10	23	The road ascends by steep zig-zags (¼ in places) for 2½ miles to crest of ridge (8,100 feet). The soil is red clay and after rain terribly slippery. It is only 4 feet wide in places. Passage of 100 mules after rain would render it impassable. Road now nearly level, running along west side of Endong—Mafi La ridge. It is terribly muddy after rain, and very liable to be blocked by falling trees. At 5 miles a series of extremely bad slips, the rock consisting of singularly friable mica schist. To keep the road open constant repairs are necessary, and then it is very unsatisfactory. At 5¾ miles, (changing place for mules) cross the Rongrong Chu, a roaring torrent, by a good bridge of two 20 feet spans. At 7¼ miles cross Chumarpo by a bridge of 15 feet span. Road then gradually descends to Samatek rest-house, 10 miles. At 7½ miles there is a flat piece of ground which, if cleared, would give a camping-ground of 50 yards by 300. This is the only level ground on this stage. Samatek is merely a clearing in the jungle.
				The road is through jungle all the way. In dry weather little water as far as Rongrong Chu. The road is very muddy nearly throughout and wears very badly. It improves near Samatek. It is only 4 feet wide in

No. of stages.	Names of stages.	DISTANCES.		REMARKS.
		Inter-mediate.	Total.	
				some six places. To stand traffic in wet weather it should be paved throughout. A regiment of Pioneers could open out this road for convoys in a day, if the weather were good, but it would take a fortnight to make it good for wet weather.
				At Samatek there is a 3-roomed rest-house, bath-room, verandah, and outhouses. A large shed is built just below. Very indifferent camping-ground for 300 men. Water plentiful; any amount of bamboo fodder. A magnificent view. Elevation by hypsometer, 6,961 feet.
				Branch Roads.
				At 8½ miles a good footpath leads down to Ringon monastery, and at the next spur another good foot-path leads down towards the Teesta valley.
3	Toong (4,400 feet).	6½	29½	The road descends at a fairly easy gradient through forest. At 2 miles cross the Tonkyong Chu by wood-en bridge 30 feet span (5,650). At 3 miles bridge over the Nim Chu. At 3¼ miles cross the Miong Chu by Iron Queen post truss bridge 45 feet span, 5 feet wide (4,550). At 5¼ miles some flattish ground suitable for a camp if cleared (500 men). At 2¾ miles cross the Ri Chu by an iron suspension bridge, 70 feet span and 4½ feet wide (4,850). Hence ¾ mile fairly level to bungalow which is situated on the hill-side some 300 feet above the river. Good 3-roomed bun-galow; shingle roof large shed for ponies and servants. No camping ground or supplies. Water, fuel, and bamboo fodder abundant.
				The road descends to the Miong Chu, after which it is up and down. It is mostly paved, though muddy in places. At present it is far too narrow in places for mule transport, though a few mules can be got along with care. A few of the gradients are bad, being as much as ¼ for short distances. The narrowness of the bridges would cause great delay and danger to con-voys. It would take a Pioneer regiment a couple of days to make the road decently passable for convoys.
				Alternative Route.
				The route from Tumlong to Toong *via* Ringon is bad and quite unsuitable for laden mules or even unladen ones.
4	Chungthang (5,070 feet)	6	35½	Steep descent of 300 feet from Toong dâk bungalow to the Teesta at Toong bridge. The bridge consists of 2 spans; one Iron Queen truss 50 feet span; and one of wood 24 feet span; each about 5 feet wide. Just above the bridge is the Toong camping ground on the right bank of the Teesta. Poor camping-ground, for 200 or 300 men. Water good and abundant. Bam-boo fodder plentiful. Large wooden shed for shel-tering animals. Road now up right bank of Teesta. Just after leaving Toong the path is through a rocky cliff and very narrow—4 feet. Opposite this the Cha-kung Chu joins the left bank of the Teesta. Passing through the cliff the road emerges into more open country at 2 miles; here there is a little cultivation and level spaces where 1,000 men could camp if the ground was cleared. Water and fuel abundant. At 3 miles the road rises rather steeply for some 300 feet and then runs fairly level for a mile through open country, and drops through forest to the level of the river. This last bit is steep and narrow — gra-dients ⅞ in places, and path 4 to 5 feet wide. Hence to Chungthang fairly level road running along just above the river; several small streams are crossed by wooden bridges; road paved in places, and in places boggy. At 5½ miles is the junction of the Lachen and Lachung rivers. The road follows the right bank of the Lachen for ¼ mile to the bridge opposite Chung-thang. The river is crossed by a strong wooden

No. of stages.	Names of stages.	DISTANCES.		REMARKS.
		Inter-mediate.	Total.	
				bridge, 32 feet span. From the bridge there is a steep ascent to the monastery of Chungthang (6 miles). There is enough ground below the monastery to camp 2,000 or 3,000 men. Some of the ground, however, is damp, and it might be unhealthy. The upper storey of the monastery has been made into a rest-house, 3 rooms. Chungthang, standing at the junction of the Lachen and Lachung valleys, is of some strategical importance, as it bars all ingress from the northern frontier of Sikkim. There are only some five houses. In its present condition the road is far too narrow for pack transport, especially at the rocky cuttings mentioned. With great care a few mules can be got over. It would take a company of Sappers and a regiment of Pioneers two days to make it suitable for large convoys.
				Alternative Route.
				The road on the left bank of the Teesta is extremely bad; several cane bridges have to be crossed. It is only suitable for foot passengers and very little used.
				Branch Route.
				From here a road leads up the Lachung valley to the Donkhya La, see Route No. 23.
5	LAMTENG (8,880 feet) .	13	48½	Road up left bank of Lachen. At 1 mile 5 or 6 acres open ground suitable for a camp. Road now rises sharply to some 300 feet above stream, which is here an impetuous torrent. The road is very steep (¼) and narrow (in places only 4 feet), passing over cliffs. Lost three mules here. Descend to river very steeply, nearly ⅓ in places. Pass two flat bits of ground at 3¼ and 4¼ miles, suitable for crossing places or small camps (250 to 300 men). At 4¾ miles bridge over side stream. At 5½ miles changing place. At 6½ miles, 200 feet below road, is a level piece of ground, camp for 300 men, nearly opposite village of Latong (6,775). Path down from new road very bad. Tukrum Chu (7¼ miles) crossed by wooden bridge. This is a roaring torrent coming straight down the hill-side. Steep ascent from bridge, then down some 400 feet to Lachen, 8½ miles; cross to right bank by light iron suspension bridge, span 90 feet, width 4½ feet (7,275). The two suspension cables are 3½ inches in circumference. Just before reaching bridge there is a nice piece of level ground, 2 or 3 acres. This might do for crossing place. At 11 miles new road from bridge has easy gradients, and winds gradually up hill-sides to some grassy downs, (8,525). Excellent camp for 2,000 men; water, fodder, and fuel in quantities. After nearly ½ mile open level ground descend 400 feet to river. At 12½ miles cross Supo Chu by good bridge, then a rise of 300 feet, after which it is level to Lamteng (13 miles).
				Lamteng contains from 60 to 70 houses. For four or five months in the year, *viz.,* November, December, April and May, the whole population of the Lachen valley live here. There is camping space for 1,000 men, and the existing houses would afford shelter to 1,000 men at a pinch. Good water and fodder in abundance. A wooden godown and kitchen afford shelter to travellers.
				The new road is too narrow for baggage animals, and some of the gradients want correcting. The hill-side presents many difficulties to making a good hill road. It is precipitous, rotten, and damp. Road should be paved throughout. Except at 11½ miles it is very damp, swarms with leeches, and is through dense jungle. Lime is found at 6¾ and 8½ miles. Spruce fir begins at about 8,000 feet. To open this stage for mule traffic would take a company of Sappers and a regiment of Pioneers two or three days.

Route No. 22—*contd.*

No. of stages.	Names of stages.	Distances.		Remarks.
		Intermediate.	Total.	
				Alternative Route.
				A very bad footpath runs up right bank of Lachen river from Chungthang. The Lachen has to be crossed by a cane bridge just above Latong, and joins new road at 6¾ miles (bridge has now broken down).
				Branch Route.
				An extremely difficult footpath leads from Lamteng over the mountains to Talung monastery, said to be three stages, *vide* Route No. 37.
6	TALLUM SAMDONG (11,450 feet).	9½	58	With the exception of one short descent the path is very fair to 3 miles, where cross Zemu river (8,900) by a good cantilever bridge, main span 66 feet, width 5 feet. River 25 yards wide, and not fordable. There is level ground close by but it is damp and requires much clearing. Junction of Zemu and Lachen rivers ½ mile below this. Steep ascent of 250 feet. Here good camping-ground for 600 or 700 men. Water and fodder procurable. Road now winds along hill-side several hundred feet above the river for 2 miles. A strong position here for resisting any attack from the north. The road now descends, and the hill-side is more open. At 5½ miles Phemakaru, a couple of sheds, and good camp for 750 to 1,000 men, near river (changing place). Path now passes along foot of a very large landslip which has partly blocked the Lachen. It is fair, but very wet and rough in places. At 6½ miles Pangri, and at 7½ miles Sirchum; a few sheds and couple of acres open ground at each. At 9¼ miles cross Lachen by a 45-foot span cantilever bridge, and at 9½ miles reach camp Tallum Samdong.
				Tallum Samdong is a summer village of 17 houses with bark roofs. There is plenty of camping-ground in the immediate neighbourhood for 1,000 men. Water, fuel, and fodder obtainable. A wooden godown and kitchen have been built for the use of travellers.
				The new road is passable for laden animals, but is rough and boggy in places.
				Branch Routes.
				There is a yak path up the left bank of the Zemu river as far as Zadang, but it does not appear to go farther. See Route No. 36.
				From Phemakaru Lachung can be reached *viâ* the Beurm La (*vide* Route No. 27). It is only a difficult footpath. No bridge at present at Phemakaru, but the Lachen can be often forded.
7	TANGU (12,750 feet)	5	63	Road all the way up left bank of Lachen, close to water, mostly over old moraine; gradients very fair. At 1½ miles Yathang, some 15 houses, and fair camping-ground. At 2½ miles cross the Yangru Chu by 20 feet bridge, a glacial stream. Here is Ka-Lep, a few houses. At 4½ miles the path goes over an open maidan, an excellent camp for 2,000 men. After crossing the Phalung Chu by a 15-foot span bridge reach Tangu village, 5 miles. Tangu is a summer village of 20 houses and the head-quarters for the feeding of yaks. There is excellent camping-ground for 2,000 men. Good water, first class grazing, and plenty of fuel. (Changing places.) A wooden godown and kitchen afford shelter to travellers.
				Branch Routes.
				From Tangu to the Naku La *viâ* the Lungna La. Laden yaks can go by this path when there is no snow. (Route No. 34.)

No. of stages.	Names of stages.	DISTANCES.		REMARKS.
		Inter-mediate.	Total.	
				From Tangu to Momay Samdong *via* the Sebu La. Only open for foot passengers. (Route No. 31.)
				From Tangu to Giaogong over the Komuthongu ridge, passable for laden yaks. (Route No. 32.)
8	GIAOGONG (15,490 feet). Height by boiling point thermometer, 15,411 feet.	9	72	Path leads up left bank of the Lachen passing through some rocks. At 1¼ miles cross to right bank by a 15-foot bridge. Here Lungna La path branches off to the left. After this path up right bank of stream all the way. It is rough and stony and in places wet. It is close to the stream and passes over the detritus from the mountains above. At 2¾ miles cross the Yangdit Chu by a 12-foot bridge. At 3¾ miles ford another glacial stream. At 6 miles there is a yak ford over the Lachen. After this the valley opens up on the right bank into a plain 2 miles long and ¼ mile wide called Sitong (14,600). A large force might be camped here; water and grazing plentiful; fuel very scarce. At 6¼ miles and 7⅓ miles cross two small glacial streams coming down from Chomiomo. At 8¼ miles camp on right bank of stream ¼ mile short of Tibetan wall at Giaogong. This road has recently been re-aligned and cleaned, and is in good order to within 2 or 3 miles of Giaogong; this remaining section will shortly be completed.
				Camping ground in abundance; water and grazing good; only yak dung for fuel.
				Giaogong is a low spur, with a stone hut and a sort of intermittent rough stone wall of no apparent use, except as a wind screen for look-out men. The Tibet-ans claim this as their frontier, and have a guard here of half a dozen men. In a rough line from this to Chomiomo they have also built bits of wall to mark their supposed boundary. Europeans are not permit-ted to cross this line. Just above Giaogong the rocky mountains entirely cease, and the hills are rounded like Wiltshire Downs. There are some conical hills to the north, 7 or 8 miles off, over 18,000 feet high, with gentle slopes. No rocks and no shrubs or trees. To the north-east the ground as far as one can see is a smooth rolling plain, gradually rising. The water parting is apparently 10 or 12 miles to the north-ward. There are absolutely no difficulties as to route, except want of fuel and the climate. To-day, 16th August, it is warm in the sun. The south wind is very cold, but no frost. Not much rain. Some of the followers complain of headache.
				Notes on the Lachen Valley.
				Population :—300 to 400 men, women, and children (Bhutias).
				Number of houses :—Lamteng—60; Tallum Samdong —15; Yathang Ka-Lep—17; Tangu—20. Below Lamteng there are no proper houses.
				Movements :—The inhabitants live at Lamteng in November and December; they then go down the valley to the villages of Latong, Tumlong, Denga, and Gnema. They return to Lamteng for April and May, and then proceed up the valley to Tallum Samdong, Yathang, Ka-Lep and Tangu, where they remain till November, then returning to Lamteng.
				Cattle :—The totals for the valley are.—yaks—400; cattle—40; ponies—100; goats—30. Two hun-dred of the yaks carry loads. In winter 100 yaks remain in Lachen and 300 go over into Tibet.
				The Tibetans are said to bring 300 yaks into the La-chen and 500 yaks and 1,000 sheep into the Lhonak valley. These numbers are very unreliable and must vary considerably. The Lachen headmen say

Route No. 22—*concld.*

No. of stages.	Names of stages.	Distances.		Remarks.
		Inter-mediate.	Total.	
				that the Tibetans used to pay a nominal rent of 7½ rupees for the use of the Lhonak valley, but that this has not been paid for some years.
				Trees :—Above 8,000 feet the conifers are conspicuous, namely, silver fir, spruce, larch and juniper, besides the yew.
				Other trees are birch, alder, ash, walnut, hazel, etc., etc. In the lower parts bamboos abound.
				Food :—Agriculture is nearly unknown ; the people practically entirely devote themselves to their yaks and cattle. They grow, however, potatoes, turnips, and a little buck-wheat.

Route No. 23.

From GANTOK to DONKHYA LA.

Authority and date.—Capt. W. F. O'Connor, R.G.A., 1900.

No. of stages	Names of stages.	Distances.		Remarks.
		Inter-mediate.	Total.	
1—4	Gantok to Chungthang	...	35½	For road from Gantok to Chungthang, see Route No. 22. Hence road lies up the Lachung river.
5	Lachung . . .	12	47½	A new road has been constructed up the right bank of the Lachung stream from Chungthang to Lachung. It is at present (September 1900) somewhat in disrepair, and laden animals could with difficulty be brought along it. For the first 3 miles the road runs almost level through an open country with patches of cultivation here and there. Opposite Chungthang and at 2½ miles the Lachung river is spanned by cane bridges. At 2¾ miles the road runs close by the river along the base of a cliff. At present the roadway has been washed away and it is necessary to strike up by a steep zig-zag path from 2⅜ miles and pass along above the cliff some 300 feet above the river. A steep muddy descent leads down again to the proper road beyond the break. Animals can be got over this path but loads would have to be taken off and carried most of the way. Road now enters forest and runs almost level for 2 miles crossing a spur some 200 feet high opposite the village of Keadum which lies on the left bank of the river. Keadum is a small village of about a dozen wooden houses standing on a flat shelf some 200 feet above the river surrounded by maize cultivation. Here and to the south of the village is camping ground for a brigade ; water, fuel, and bamboo fodder plentiful. The road to Lachung continues along the right bank through forest. One mile beyond Keadum the river is spanned by a wooden cantilever bridge 90 feet in length, 4½ feet wide, and 15 feet above the water level. The actual width of the stream here is some 50 feet. The current is swift and unfordable. A path from the road under report leads to this bridge and hence to Keadum. At 6 miles from Chungthang the road emerges from forest at Liuten and runs almost level through open grassy flats with patches of jungle here and there to the Bi Chu at 9 miles. This is a small mountain torrent crossed by a ricketty wooden bridge. The stream is fordable being about 2½ feet deep—current swift. It might be dangerous when in flood.

No. of stages.	Names of stages.	DISTANCES.		REMARKS.
		Inter-mediate.	Total.	
				A steep rise leads to an open plateau across which the road runs; and in 3 miles Lachung village is reached, the road passing through an open stretch of grassy country, rising and falling over the spurs from the hill-sides to the west. This part of the road is in places rough and sometimes swampy but offers no serious difficulties. Lachung village lies on the left bank of the stream which is crossed by a wooden cantilever bridge, 132 feet long with a 4-foot roadway, some 15 feet above the level of the stream. Stream swift and unfordable.
				Lachung village contains about 70 houses, the larger number being on the left bank of the river. It occupies a gentle slope below an open grassy terminal moraine. The houses, each of which stands in a low stone-wall enclosure, are substantially built on a foundation of loosely piled stones, in which are embedded the main beams; the upper stories are of wood, plastered over with mud, the roofs being of shingles kept in place by large stones; the lower stories would form good godowns, while the upper might be employed as barracks for troops. The houses as a whole are large, the biggest being 39×21 feet outside measurement.
				The supplies available are about 200 cattle and yaks scattered about the valley and a few turnips. There are also about a dozen ponies in the village which would be available for transport purposes.
				There is also a large store of Indian corn in the village after the harvest, which is gradually consumed during the winter months.
				The general direction of the Lachung valley at Lachung is east and west; the river flows in a broad stony bed, the right bank rising gently from the water's edge for 200 yards when the hill shoots up in a series of steep grass slopes and rock precipices some 3,000 feet higher; the left bank rises in a gravel precipice about 30 feet high and then slopes away very gently to the spurs running down from the Thanka La. Except at Lachung itself and the range bounding the Thanka La valley on the east, the hills on the left bank of the Lachung are thickly wooded with fir forest, and are generally steep.
				To the west of the village on the left bank of the river is an extensive open flat on which a brigade could easily encamp; a stream of excellent water fully sufficient for the requirements of a force of the above size flows across the flat. In fact camping-ground about Lachung is unlimited if the flats towards the Bi Chu are included. Fuel is plentiful. Lachung, elevation 8,836 feet, has a much drier climate than any spot further south in Sikkim. The hills for ½ a mile on all sides of the village are open, and beyond this are alternate open stretches and patches of fir forest; the lower slopes are gentle, but above they become rocky and precipitous and ascend rapidly to the snows.
7	YUMTHANG . . .	10	57½	Cross from Lachung village to the left bank of the Lachung river by the bridge described above. The road is a rough track winding amongst stones and boulders and rising gradually to the hamlet of Na-mo-na-sa, at 2 miles, near the junction of the Sebu Chu* with the Lachung. Here a road branches off to the right crossing the Lachung by a wooden brige and leading to the Ghora La (see Route No. 28).
				At 3 miles a steep rise of 700 feet through forest leads to the summit of a moraine across the top of which track runs level for ½ mile and then descends steeply on the other side. Up to this point the track is bad and broken—boggy in some places and rocky in others. Hence to Yumthang it is rather better. It crosses a wide open maidan, almost level, from 4th to 5th mile,

* There is another Sebu Chu which joins the Lachung near Momay Samdong.

Route No. 23—*contd.*

No. of stages.	Names of stages.	Distances.		Remarks.
		Intermediate.	Total.	
				and passes over a steep moraine at 5½ miles. At the 6th mile a stream is crossed the largest of those met along the road—2 ft. deep, sluggish current, sandy bottom. Beyond this the valley is open level and grassy, the Lachung river flowing close under the hills on the east. A short ascent and descent lead into the Yumthang plain which is a wide open valley some 2 miles in length, and from ¼ to ½ a mile wide. Through this the river meanders, winding from side to side.
				Yumthang village lies about ⅓ of the way up this valley and is a small village consisting of some 20 or 30 wooden houses. It is a grazing station for the Lachung people when they bring their yaks, sheep, and goats in summer.
				Camping ground practically unlimited. Water and fuel abundant. Fodder scanty; animals could find grazing on the maidan. Elevation of Yumthang, 11,650 ft.
				One mile short of Yumthang there is a hot spring on the left bank of the Lachung. Temperature of the water 114° 5F.
8	MOMAY SAMDONG	9	66½	Follow the path along the right bank of the Lachung for 500 yards to a wooden cantilever bridge which here crosses the stream. Strong bridge, fit for laden animals, 50 feet span. Stream fordable just below the bridge; depth 3 feet; current gentle; bottom pebbly.
				From the bridge a path continues up the right bank of the Lachung leading eventually across the Beurm La into the Lachen valley (*vide* Route No. 27).
				The road to Momay Samdong now runs level for 1 mile up the left bank of the stream and then enters forest. Hence to 3 miles the track is up and down through forest; very rough going. At 3 miles cross the Lachung again by a wooden cantilever bridge, 60 feet span, strong enough to take animals. Stream very swift and unfordable. Elevation here 12,500 feet.
				From this bridge there is a long steep rise of 1,000 feet, gradient ¼. Hence steady ascent to an elevation of 14,000 feet. After this elevation the larger scrub jungle is left behind, but small bushes of juniper and rhododendron sufficient for fuel are found to within one mile of Momay Samdong. For the last 3 miles the road is almost level, rising very gradually to the stream flowing from the Sebu La.* Ford this stream opposit Samdong. The stream is about 2½ feet deep; current swift; stony bottom. There is a small temporary wooden bridge for foot passengers.
				Momay Samdong is a wide grassy expanse at the junction of 3 streams; one coming from the Sebu La; one from the Donkhya La (this is the main stream); and the third, the Temba Chu, from the snows of the Chumbi frontier. There are 6 or 7 scattered houses; built of stone with shingle roofs. Practically unlimited camping ground on firm level grassy soil. No fuel except yak dung within one mile. Water plentiful. Scanty grass for fodder.
				Momay Samdong is one of the highest grazing grounds in Sikkim, and during September and October nearly all the Lachung yaks are found here.
				Elevation by hypsometer 15,587 feet. It may be noted here that this place is known to the natives as "Samdong". The word "Momay" is not in use amongst them.
	DONKHYA LA	9½	76	From Momay Samdong the path runs up the right bank of the Lachung for ⅓ mile, when the stream is forded; water 1½ feet. deep; breadth of stream 45 feet; bottom

* There is another Sebu La (also known as Sebubu La) on the road north from Giaogong to Kamba Jong.

Route No. 23—*contd.*

No. of stages.	Names of stages.	Distances.		Remarks.
		Inter-mediate.	Total.	
				stony; current swift. There is a temporary wooden foot-bridge for passengers. Path now continues up the left bank to 4 miles. It is a fairly level track keeping generally close to the river, rising at times 100 feet above it. There is no roadway—a mere rough track winding amongst rocks; boggy in places. At 4 miles the river is again crossed by a ford 1 foot deep; current gentle; stony bottom. The stream is here some 30 or 40 yards in width.
				The road now runs up the right bank through an open almost level valley keeping some 500 to 600 yards from the river and 100 to 200 feet above it. At 7 miles a steep rise to the left (west) leads on to the summit of an elevated plateau (16,200 feet) overlooking the Donkhya La, due north. The lowest depression in the range lies a little to the left (west) of the actual pass and the approach to it is difficult up a steep stone shoot. This saddle appears at first sight to be the pass, but the track leading to the Donkhya La can be seen from here and defines the spot where the ridge is crossed. Donkhya Ri (or mountain) lies north-north-east by east from here; it is a huge pillar of rock rising to a height of 20,260 feet, snow capped and absolutely precipitous on the south and east. Immediately to the west of this mountain, and about ¾ mile east of the Donkhya pass another low saddle is seen in the ridge. This is the Karpo La and will be found reported on in Route No. 23(a).
				From this plateau to Donkhya La is 2 miles; the first 1½ easy, descending gradually to the foot of the steep rise which leads to the pass. Two or three small lakes are passed. A steady ascent now begins and for a rise of some 200 feet the gradient is easy, the path winding up the face of the ridge. At 150 feet from the summit there is a flat shelf where the Tibetans have built a small defence wall which commands the path leading up to the pass. It is a 5-foot loopholed wall some 40 yards in length, in bad repair. It can be overlooked and outflanked from a spur on the east some 500 yards distant.
				Hence to summit of pass a steep pull of 150 feet. A defence wall built by the Tibetans runs along the whole crest of the ridge extending for about 100 yards up the slopes to the east of the pass and for 300 or 400 yards down those to the west. There is a gap at the actual pass for traffic. It is a strong 6-foot loopholed wall, some 2 feet in thickness and in pretty good repair. This wall also can be outflanked from the spur to the east mentioned above.
				From the top of the Donkhya pass a fine view can be obtained into Tibet. Immediately below the pass lie the Cholamo lakes which are drained by a stream from their northern margin. This stream running north joins a larger stream coming from the east, and the two united flow north-west out of sight round a projecting spur. This stream flowing west along the frontier and turning south near Giaogong is the head waters of the Lachen, or Teesta river. The actual source of the stream lies further east, rising on slopes invisible from this part of the frontier. North of the Cholamo lakes the country presents the barren appearance of the usual Tibetan landscape. Low bare hills some 10 or 12 miles away appear to form the water-shed of the Lachen river; the valley of the Yaru Chu lying beyond. In the far distance are seen the mountains of the great central Himalayan chain running east and west as far as the eye can reach. They are but sparsely covered with snow. Due north a very high snow peak rises abruptly; but from north to north-west the range is altogether free of snow. West of this again snow peaks occur to the limit of view. From this great elevation these mountains appear insignificant; but the higher peaks rise probably to 22,000 or 23,000 feet. Generally speaking their

Route No. 23—*concld.*

No. of stages.	Names of stages.	DISTANCES.		REMARKS.
		Inter-mediate.	Total.	
				outline is rounded and the slopes appear easy. They could probably be crossed in many places. Two passes are known to the immediate north of Sikkim—(*vide* Tibetan Routes Nos. 2 and 3).
				The watershed of several of the Indian rivers (the Arun, Gandak, and others) is on the southern slopes of this range; that of the Brahmaputra on the northern.
				Elevation of summit of pass 18,100 feet.
				The Tibetan guard which is stationed here to watch the pass, have their quarters in the plain below, some 2 or 3 miles distant.

Route No. 23(*a*).

From MOMAY SAMDONG to KARPO LA.

Authority and date.—Capt. W. F. O'Connor, R.G.A., 1900.

No. of stages.	Names of stages.	DISTANCES.		REMARKS.
		Inter-mediate.	Total.	
1	Karpo La	9	9	Follow the road to Donkhya La for 7 miles and ascend to the summit of the plateau mentioned in Route No. 23 whence a view can be obtained of the Donkhya La, Karpo La, and the hills in their vicinity. From here the Karpo La lies N.-N.-E., immediately to the west of the Donkhya mountain, and east of the Donkhya La, separated from the latter by a steep stony hill. The pass is a well-marked saddle in the ridge.
				From the plateau to the foot of the pass is easy going over open undulating ground. A slight descent leads to a small lake; skirt the western margin of the lake and at 1½ miles from the plateau another small lakelet is reached. At this point there is some difficult going and the ground is impassable for animals as there are piles of boulders scattered round the margin of the lake which must be crossed to reach the pass. These boulders are easily passed by men on foot but would be dangerous for animals. Hence ascent to top of pass is an easy slope of 300 feet.
				A fine view into Tibet is obtained from the summit. Immediately below the pass is a small lake some 200 feet lower down. A stream coming from the east runs into the lake, and flows out again from the north-west corner, continuing its course to join the stream draining the Cholamo lakes as mentioned in Route No. 23. In the far distance appears the range of the Central Himalayan chain; a gap in the chain bearing north-north-east by north looks easy, free from snow and approached apparently by a gentle gradient.
				In the plain beyond the foot of the pass was a *dok* or encampment of Tibetan herdsmen; and some hundreds of yaks and sheep were seen grazing here and there. Elevation of pass 17,918 feet by hypsometer. The descent into Tibet appears easy over a field of frozen snow sloping gently to the foot of the pass some 200 feet below.
				This pass might prove extremely useful as a means of turning the Donkhya pass should such a thing be necessary. The approach to the pass is out of sight

Route No. 23(*a*)—*concld.*

No. of stages.	Names of stages.	DISTANCES.		REMARKS.
		Inter-mediate.	Total.	
				from the Donkhya, and a few men despatched over the Karpo La could easily descend into Tibet and take the defenders of the Donkhya in the rear.
				There being no name in use amongst the natives for this pass it has been christened the Karpo La, or "white pass," from the colour of the slope leading up to the top on the Sikkim side. The people of the Lachung valley were informed of this name.
				The name of the stream flowing from the east into the small lake at the foot of the pass on the Tibetan side is said to be Gyadong Chu.

Route No. 24.

FROM GANTOK TO PAMIONCHI, *via* SONG.

Authority and dates.—POLITICAL OFFICER, SIKKIM, 1897.

No. of stages.	Names of stages.	DISTANCES.		REMARKS.
		Inter-mediate.	Total.	
1 & 2	SONG AND TEMI	...	26	See Route No. 6.
3	KEUZING	8	34	Follow Route No. 6 up the spur, entering thick forest near the summit of the mountain until the road turning south to Namchi is reached at Damthang. Here turn right and follow the road which runs all through forest along the crest of the ridge, ascending and descending *via* the peaks called Rufu La and Timbi La. Road good. From Timbi La descend for about 2 miles through forest. After this cultivation is reached, and the hill-sides are cleared and dotted with houses. Keuzing is a good camping ground below the road which could contain two battalions; two streams run through the camp; fodder 1 mile down hill; *no bazar*; no supplies obtainable, except in very small quantities; no water along this road between Temi and Keuzing.
				This portion of the road is unmetalled, and in wet weather becomes very heavy, especially when it runs along the summit of the ridge. It is, however, passable for baggage animals.
				There is no dâk bungalow at Keuzing, but shelter may be obtained in the house of Kazi Jerung, the local landlord.
4	PAMIONCHI	9	43	The descent to the Rangit at Ligsip is very steep. Here there is a small dâk bungalow; a wooden hut only, with 2 small rooms; no furniture. The river is crossed by a galvanized steel suspension bridge 160 feet long, 4½ feet roadway. The river is quite unfordable, the bottom strewn with great boulders. Hence ascend to Pamionchi, for which road, *vide* Route No. 8, Stage 3. This road is steep, but in good order.

Route No. 25.

From GANTOK to NAKU LA *via* Talung.

Authority and date.—Political Officer, Sikkim, 1892 and 1894.

No. of stages.	Names of stages.	Distances.		Remarks.
		Intermediate.	Total.	
1	Tumlong	14	14	For this stage, *vide* Route No. 22, Stage 2.
2	Maling	18	32	Follow the Tumlong-Samatek road for about 10 miles, and then turn down a path leading down the crest of a ridge to the Teesta, *vide* Route No. 11.
3 & 4	Be	...	..	Cross the Teesta by a cane bridge, and afterwards the Thalung Chu by ditto. Road up left bank of Talung Chu, passing several small hamlets. Rindiang Chu crossed by wooden bridge opposite Be. From Be a road runs to Jongri *via* the Guicha La, *vide* Route No. 38.
5	Talung	...	...	Good road to Talung Monastery along the right bank of the Rindiang, which runs in deep rocky gorges. Talung is one of the oldest monasteries in Sikkim, and is rarely visited. From Talung a path goes to Lamteng *via* the Tukcham La, *vide* Route No. 37.
6 to 8	Yumtso La	...	...	Three days' march; the road still runs up the river, and is easy. At Tizong, elevation 10,200 feet, fir trees cease to grow, and a steep hill is climbed, on which snow may be found in patches in June. Two lakes are passed on the way to the summit of the Yumtso pass, which lies at an elevation of 15,800 feet. Ascent easy.
9	Thang-chung	...	...	The descent from the Yumtso pass is easy if the road is free from snow, but before reaching the camping-ground at Thang-chung the foot of the great glacier from Kangchenjunga has to be crossed; here the road is bad and difficult.
10 & 11	Naku La	...	...	Two days' march—the first over the Thang-chung La to the Tumrachen Chu, and the second over the The La, elevation, 16,575 feet, into Lho Nak. There are no difficulties on the road provided the passes are free from snow. The descent from The La is by a well-marked yak track, first over steep stony ground; at 16,000 feet is a small lake in a level basin, and thence track lies down a little stream, the sides of which are fringed with bushes. This stream runs into the Langpo Chu which is crossed with some difficulty, the current being strong and the bottom stony, depth about 3 feet. However, laden coolies can be got across with the help of a rope. Hence to Naku La, see Routes Nos. 34 and 35. This road is used by the inhabitants of Be and Talung, who trade with Tibet. Numbers of yaks and sheep pass over it, so the track is well-defined. From the summit of the The La a fine view is obtained northwards towards the Naku La.

Route No. 26.

From LACHUNG to THANKA LA.

Authority and date.—Surgeon-Captain A. Pearse, A.M.S., December 1896.

No. of stages.	Names of stages.	Distances.		Remarks.
		Intermediate.	Total.	
1	Jukyak	9	9	Leaving the village of Lachung on the east, the road rises 800 feet in about half a mile over grassy slopes; then, passing along the top of a small ridge through

Route No. 26—*concld.*

No. of stages.	Names of stages.	Distances.		Remarks.
		Intermediate.	Total.	
				a patch of pine forest for half a mile, emerges on the open side of the main ridge along which it runs to two miles. This slope of the ridge is covered with grass, and is very steep, the angle from the road to the river, 600 feet below, being as much as 45° in most places. At 2 miles pine forests are entered, and at 3½ miles (elevation 10,900 feet) a stream is crossed by ford. At six miles Mempoopya, a small open place, capable of affording camping-ground for about 50 men (fuel and fodder abundant; water ¼ mile distant) is reached. At 8 miles the road leaves the forest and passes through rhododendron scrub to Jukyak (elevation 12,800 feet) at 9 miles.
				At Jukyak camping-ground can be found on the north side of the valley, but it is not good, though fuel, water, and fodder are abundant.
2	Chungpya . . .	7½	16½	For three miles the road passes along the right bank of the river by easy gradient through rhododendron scrub. At 3 miles there is a very steep and precipitous ascent to 3½ miles, where the road passes through a gorge (Chumbocum) 150 yards long by 20—30 yards broad, the river being to the east and in the same gorge at a lower level. At the northern end of the gorge (elevation 14,800 feet) the river is crossed by ford, and the road then passes along its left bank by easy gradients till an elevation of 15,200 feet is reached at 6 miles. It then leaves the river and passes by easy gradient between two ridges to Chungpya (elevation 15,500 feet) at 7½ miles.
				At Chungpya coolies halt for the night previous to crossing the pass the following day. There is no ground for camping troops.
	Thanka La . . .	1¼	17¾	From Chungpya there is a steep rocky ascent for one mile succeeded by practically level ground for ¼ of a mile to the summit of the pass (elevation 16,400 feet). On the Tibetan side the descent is very precipitous for about 2 miles over rough, rocky ground. At 2 miles there is a small lake from which the river flows. The road crosses the pass due north and south, but on the Tibetan side passes down the valley south-south-east to Chumbi.
				NOTE.—The general direction of the road is south-east, it is not practicable for laden animals, and is little used by coolies.

Route No. 26 (*a*).

FROM CHUMBOCUM GORGE TO PATO LA.

Authority and date.—SURGEON-CAPTAIN A. PEARSE, A.M.S., DECEMBER 1896.

No. of stages.	Names of stages.	Distances.		Remarks.
		Intermediate.	Total.	
1	Pato La . . .	10	10	The general direction of the road is north-east. It leaves that to the Thanka La immediately on its exit from the gorge, and runs north-east over rough, rocky ground for 2 miles; it then ascends and crosses a high ridge joining a road which ascends the Semo Chu valley from Dombong. The Pato La is said to be an easy pass and slightly higher than the Thanka La (Surgeon-Captain Pearse had only been a short distance along the road to it).

Route No. 27.

From LACHUNG to LAMTENG *via* BEURM LA.

Authority and date.—Lieut. W. F. O'Connor, R.A., 1895.

No. of stages	Names of stages.	Distances.		Remarks.
		Intermediate.	Total.	
1	Yumthang	10	10	*Vide* Route No. 23.
2	Lako	9	19	About ½ a mile above the village of Yumthang the road north to Momay Samdong and the Donkhya La crosses the river by a wooden cantilever bridge, 50 feet long, capable of bearing ponies or mules, but the river is easily fordable below the bridge, being about 3 feet in depth, with a pebbly bottom and gentle current.
				The road to Lako is level, following the right bank of the river for the first mile and a half. It then crosses a stream which comes down a small valley on the west of the main valley, and turns westwards up through the forest; it is a mere cattle track used by the people of the valley to take their yaks up to the higher pasturage; the ascent is steep, about 1,000 feet in the mile. The forest consists of pine and rhododendron up to 12,000 feet, and from 12,000 to 13,000 of very fine juniper trees. At 13,000 feet the large juniper is left behind, and the track is traced through rhododendron and juniper scrub. From 14,000 feet all jungle is left behind, and the path winds among large rocks with patches of coarse herbage here and there, where the yaks graze. The camping-ground at 14,700 feet is at the bottom of a long slope, which runs up steeply to the north-west to a height of about 15,500 feet, crowned by rugged crags and small glaciers coming from snow fields high above.
				Space available for camping is about 400 yards by 200 yards. The ground is covered with stones and coarse herbage. Large rocks in the vicinity give excellent shelter for the coolies. Rhododendron fuel must be carried up from 700 feet lower down.
				Lako is 14,700 feet above sea-level.
3	Beurm	6	25	The road leads first up a steep moraine, due west, about 400 feet high, at the top of which is found a small glacier, about 300 yards across, which can be easily climbed and crossed, the top being fairly level and undulating and free from crevasses. From here two roads lead over the range of mountains to the west, across two saddles, meeting again on the opposite side.
				One, due west, and crowned by jagged peaks of rock, appears the lowest, and the natives say is the easiest; by this they sometimes drive their yaks into the opposite valley.
				The other, which our party crossed, lies more to the south, and is said to be the shortest. It is reached by a steep stony ravine, the summit of the pass (the Beurm La) being 16,100 feet. Thence a steep and rocky descent of 400 feet leads to a level maidan, about ½ mile long by 200 or 300 yards wide, on the further side of which is a large glacier coming from the snows to the north-west. The way lies across the glacier, which presents no difficulties, and from the opposite side down the valley through a ravine with perpendicular sides, general direction south-west. Beyond the ravine the valley is level and rocky for about one mile, when a grassy flat is reached, called by the natives "Beurm." This flat, which is about 500 yards square, forms an excellent camping ground, with abundance of water and scrub juniper and rhododendron for fuel, and large overhanging rocks as coolie shelter. Beurm is 14,450 feet above sea-level.

No. of stages.	Names of stages.	DISTANCES.		REMARKS.
		Inter-mediate.	Total,	
4	PHEMA KARU . .	10	35	The road runs through a long narrow valley, general direction south-west. On both sides of the stream ancient moraines rise to a height of 500 feet, which are evidently subject to constant stone avalanches, but the bottom of the valley, though stony, is free from jungle for the entire distance, and slopes easily, until within 2 miles of Phema Karu, when a gorge with precipitous sides is reached, which would be quite impracticable for animals, and requires some stiff climbing to get down at all.
				On starting the right bank of the stream is followed. On reaching an elevation of about 12,000 feet the stream should be crossed, which can here be done without difficulty, and the left bank followed until the gorge just spoken of is passed. Here the stream must again be crossed, for which purpose a small bridge (20 feet long) can easily be made with the fir trees which grow close by. This stream, which is unnamed on the maps, is called the Beurm Chu, and debouches just below Phema Karu into the Lachen river ; it is here about 20 feet wide, and nowhere more than 4 feet deep, but quite unfordable owing to the speed of the current and the boulders in the bed of the stream.
				A path will now be found through jungle leading in a north-west direction over the spur down to the Lachen river, which is crossed by a rough bridge opposite Phema Karu. The Lachen is here about 50 or 60 yards in width, and in places 6 or 8 feet deep. The bridge is formed by fallen trees with a tangle of brushwood in the centre, and is the result of a landslip which occurred about nine years ago. It is passable only for men, and then with the aid of a slight hand-rail, as in places the torrent rushes over the tree trunks to the height of a foot or more.
				Phema Karu is 10,200 feet above sea-level, and consists of a few wooden sheds on a level grassy spot some ½ mile square on the right bank of the Lachen river. It forms a good camping-ground, fuel and water being plentiful and close. The people of the valley graze their sheep, cattle, and yaks two or three marches to the north, during the summer months, so that milk, butter, and meat can be procured with little difficulty.
				Phema Karu is the "Praimkar" of the north-east trans-frontier of India map.
5	LAMTENG . . .	6	41	For this march see Route No. 22.
				The Beurm La is a pass of some importance as a rapid means of communication between the Lachung and Lachen valleys, as a native messenger can cross from Phema Karu to Yumthang in one day or from Lamteng to Lachung village in two; but it is quite unfitted for animal transport of any kind or for troops, except in small numbers, or on an emergency when it would be necessary to construct a bridge of some kind across the Lachen river.
				NOTE.—The distances given are approximate only. Elevations by aneroid barometer.

Route No. 28.

From LACHUNG to GHORA LA.

Authority and date.—Surgeon-Captain A. Pearse, A. M. S., December 1896.

No. of stages.	Names of stages.	Distances.		Remarks.
		Inter-mediate.	Total.	
				The general direction of the road is north-west.
1	Dombong . . .	8	8	This road leaves that to the Donkhya La, about 2½ miles above Lachung on its eastern side, and passing through more or less open jungle crosses the Lachung river by a good wooden bridge at 3 miles. The banks of the river at this point are about 40 feet high and precipitous. The road, which is rough, then rises steadily by easy gradients to Seyroom (elevation 10,200 feet) at 5 miles. Seyroom is on the Sebo Chu, and affords good camping-ground on both sides of the river, with abundance of fuel, fodder, and water. The road here is practically level for half a mile along the right bank of the river; it then becomes rather rough and steep for a mile, when another flat open bit of country is reached, which extends on both sides of the river to Dombong at 8 miles. At Dombong (elevation 10,500 feet) there are about 12 or 15 Bhootia huts and good camping-ground of considerable size on both sides of the river. Fuel, fodder, and water abundant.
2	Tukpoo Memo . .	11	19	From Dombong the road ascends by easy gradients for one mile; it then becomes exceedingly steep, and is overhung by cliffs 400—500 feet high for half a mile. From one and a half miles it passes through open pine forest by easy gradient, crossing two small streams, to Sebo Memo (elevation 11,900 feet) at 5 miles. Here there is an artificial clearing in the forest and six or eight Bhootia huts and good camping-ground. After passing through more pine forests by easy gradient Sebo Como (elevation 12,000 feet) is reached at 5½ miles. Sebo Como is very similar to Sebo Memo, but contains only three Bhootia huts. The road leaves the pine forest at 9 miles, and then passes through rhododendron jungle along the right bank of the Sebo Chu to Tukpoo Memo at 11 miles, the gradient being easy throughout. At Tukpoo Memo there are Bhootia huts, good ground for camping on both sides of the river, with abundance of fuel, fodder, and water.
3	Sethang . . .	5½	24½	From Tukpoo Memo to Tukpoo Como the road passes through rhododendron scrub; it is rough in places, but the gradient is easy. The valley is from ½ to 1½ miles broad, the mountain sides being steep and in places precipitous. About 300 yards below Tukpoo Como the Phegoo Chu is crossed by a plank bridge. It can also be forded 150 yards higher up. At Tukpoo Como (elevation 13,800 feet) there are three or four stone huts and a large open space for camping, but the ground is said to be very marshy in the rains owing to its being situated on the tongue of land between the Sebo Chu and Phegoo Chu (the map referred to below is incorrect as regards the Tocklung Chu, *A. Pearse*) which join about ¼ of a mile below. From Tukpoo Como there is a steep rocky ascent of 600 feet in a mile to Sethang at 5½ miles. Sethang is situated on a grassy plateau (200 × 300 yards) surrounded by rocks, and affords excellent camping-ground.
4	Nairkung . . .	6½	31	The road leaves Sethang in a north-easterly direction, and at about 400 yards it crosses the Sebo Chen Chu by a narrow plank bridge 7 feet long and 30 feet above the river, which here runs in a very narrow gorge, elevation above sea-level being 14,800 feet. It then winds by a steep rocky ascent to Chuchaki (elevation 15,100 feet) at 1½ miles; here it emerges on a flat marshy piece of ground (200 × 400 yards) through which the Sebo Chung Chu flows. Having skirted the western margin of the marsh the road ascends a steep ridge from its north-western corner to an elevation of 15,500 feet at 2½ miles. It then passes along the side of the mountain by very easy gradient, and at 5½ miles

Route No. 28—*concld.*

No. of stages.	Names of stages.	DISTANCES.		REMARKS.
		Inter-mediate.	Total.	
				the yak grazing station of Tukpoochi is reached, and that of Nairkung at 6½ miles, each having an elevation of 15,700 feet above sea-level. At each place there are some eight or ten huts (stone), excellent ground for camping, with abundance of water and grazing, but no fuel.
				Alternative Route.
				This passes in a northerly direction from Sethang and is steep and rocky for half a mile, and rises 300 feet in this distance. It then runs along the right bank of the Sebo Chen Chu, crossing it by ford at 1½ miles (elevation 15,200 feet), the river being 10 yards broad and 18 inches deep (in November). The road then ascends steeply along the side of the mountain to join the former route at the point (elevation 15,500 feet), where it leaves the crest of the ridge above Chuchaki.
				This latter route is the easier and apparently more frequented. It is 1½ miles longer, but less rocky and the gradients less steep.
5	GHORA LA . . .	5	36	Immediately below Nairkung two streams join to form the Sebo Chung Chu. Neither of the streams are visible above their junction in November, but the water can be heard some 2 or 3 feet below the surface of the ground. The road crosses the northernmost stream, about 150 yards from Nairkung, and divides.
				The road passes along the right bank of the southern stream by very easy gradient to one mile, where the foot of a glacier is reached; it then passes along the ridge separating the two streams near the edge of the glacier to 2 miles, when it rises very steeply to pass through a gap in the ridge to the glacier on the opposite side, along the surface of which it passes for about 300 yards to the summit of the pass at 36 miles.
				An alternative route passes along the northern branch of the Sebo Chung Chu, the gradient being easy, to the edge of a shallow lake at one mile. It skirts the edge of this lake for ¾ of a mile, and then passes towards the glacier, near the foot of which it runs in a northerly direction to the lateral moraine, along which it ascends to 3 miles where it passes on to the glacier, and by a somewhat steep ascent reaches the top of the pass at 36½ miles.
				NOTE.—The road to the Ghora La is easy for coolies throughout, except over the glacier. It is also practicable for baggage animals when laden, except at the following places, *viz.*, the banks of the Lachung river, from 7½ to 8 miles, from 13½ to 14½ miles, from Tukpoo Como to Sethang by alternative route, from Tukpoo Como to Chuchaki and from the foot of the glacier to the summit of the pass. The natives state that yaks and ponies can cross the pass in the rains. On 14th November 1896 water boiled at 182·2° F. at 4-15 P.M. at the top of the Ghora La. Elevation by aneroid barometer was 17,900 feet.
				Surgeon-Captain Pearse is of opinion that the Ghora La is situated some 8 miles further north than is shown in Sheet No. 7 $\frac{\text{N. W.}}{\text{I.}}$ and part of 6 $\frac{\text{S. W.}}{3}$ of the north-east trans-frontier of India map, 1879—1884.

Route No. 28(*a*).

FROM TUKPOO COMO TO SETHANG *viâ* CHEYCHIMA.

Authority and date.—SURGEON-CAPTAIN A. PEARSE, A.M.S., DECEMBER 1896.

No. of stages.	Names of stages.	DISTANCES.		REMARKS.
		Inter-mediate.	Total.	
1	CHEYCHIMA . . .	6	6	Leaving Tukpoo Como to the west the road immediately ascends by numerous short zig-zags for ¾ of a mile, rising 800 feet in this distance. It then emerges on the wide open valley of the Phegoo Chu and follows the left bank of this stream, rising steadily by easy gradient to Cheychima at 6 miles, an elevation of 15,250 feet. At Cheychima there are three stone huts, with considerable ground for camping ; water and grazing abundant, and fuel (rhododendron scrub) can be obtained about two miles below along the right bank of the Phegoo Chu.
2	SETHANG . . .	8	14	From Cheychima the road runs east-north-east up a steep ridge to 2 miles, rising 1,000 feet, and then winds round the ridge passing near the foot of a large glacier to 3½ miles. It then rises steeply to the top of the ridge overlooking Sethang at 4 miles. From the top of the ridge (elevation 16,600 feet) the descent is very precipitous to 5 miles, becoming less steep as it descends. From 6—7 miles, where it joins the road to the Ghora La, it is practically level. The road is not practicable for animals, and in places difficult for coolies.

Route No. 29.

FROM LACHUNG TO MOMAY SAMDONG *viâ* CHEYCHIMA.

Authority and date.—SURGEON-CAPTAIN A. PEARSE, A.M.S., DECEMBER 1896.

No. of stages.	Names of stages.	DISTANCES.		REMARKS.
		Inter-mediate.	Total.	
1 to 3	CHEYCHIMA . . .	...	...	For road from Lachung to Cheychima, see Routes Nos. 28 and 28(*a*).
4 and 5	MOMAY SAMDONG . .	...	...	From Cheychima to Momay Samdong is a two days' march. The road runs north by easy gradient to 2 miles, where the river is crossed by ford. It then rises along the crest of a ridge for 300 feet over rocky ground, emerging on a sandy plateau through which the Phegoo Chu flows. It then follows the right bank of the stream for 2½ miles (5 miles from Cheychima), going in a north-westerly direction to cross the ridge at 6½ miles which separates this valley from that of the Temba Chu. There is a small glacier at the top of the ridge. From Cheychima to the foot of the glacier is passable for baggage animals.

Route No. 30.

From GIAOGONG to DONKHYA LA, *via* CHOLAMO LAKES.

Authority and date.—Surgeon-Captain A. Pearse, A.M.S., December 1896.

No. of stages.	Names of stages.	Distances.		Remarks.
		Inter-mediate.	Total.	
				General direction, east.
1	Donkhya La	18	18	After passing Giaogong, where there is a loop-holed wall which stretches completely across the valley, the road is practically level, and runs almost due north for 2 miles to the Lachen river. The river is crossed by a shallow ford, and the road then runs eastward along its bank over slightly undulating country for some 8 miles. For 5 miles the ground is covered with short grass, but then becomes more or less pebbly or sandy. The whole valley is perfectly open, with a few large rocks here and there, and even off the beaten track easy for transport animals. On both sides of the river there is good camping-ground, abundance of water, good grazing in places, but no fuel. The whole country along the river appeared to be of a character similar to that of the first 8 miles from Giaogong.
				At 4 miles from the top of the pass the road skirts the northern and north-western margins of the Cholamo lakes, and hence rises gradually towards the pass. For the last 2½ miles the ascent is steep, and the road rough and rocky.
				Laden yaks and ponies pass over the Donkhya La which is situated at an elevation of 18,550 feet by aneroid barometer.

Route No. 31.

From GIAOGONG to MOMAY SAMDONG, *via* SEBU LA.

Authority.—Brigadier-General A. G. Yeatman-Biggs, C.B., August 1896.

No. of stages.	Names of stages.	Distances.		Remarks.
		Inter-mediate.	Total.	
1	Camp, foot of Sebu La (15,400 feet).	8½	8½	After leaving camp Giaogong cross to left bank of Lachen river, ascend the slope of the hill obliquely in a generally southerly direction, passing the south end of a small lake and up a smart rise to the shoulder of the ragged ridge which ends at Giaogong. This shoulder (3 miles) is much used as a track. The Tibetans have built here a double dry stone wall, 4 feet high. The position is good, but the wall absurd. The shoulder or pass is called Gyubgi-La (16,650). The road now winds to the left round the shoulder and descends to a rocky, grassy valley. At the bottom is a lake and a pond (15,800) just south of the track. The track keeps to the left on the higher ground. From the pond the track runs east till a second spur is crossed (16,850). This is the highest point in the march. From hence down a long, grassy, rocky valley, a wide bed of an ancient glacial stream, with high moraine hills on the right and a rocky ridge to the left. At about 1 mile from head of valley cross glacial stream to left bank (5 miles). Here is a dry lake with curious sluice-like exit. Here another stream comes down a ravine at right angles, and after crossing this the track bears away to the left, in the direction of the north end of the rocky range in front.

Route No. 31—*concld.*

No. of stages.	Names of stages.	DISTANCES.		REMARKS.
		Inter-mediate.	Total.	
				An enormous grassy moraine is now crossed with a very steep descent into the valley of the Phalung Chu (15,000). On arriving at the stream ride up the right bank to a good camp just at the foot of the Sebu La (15,400), 8½ miles.
2	MOMAY SAMDONG (15,587 feet).	9	17½	The first start from camp is to cross the stream and climb the almost vertical slope to the first ridge, the rise being 600 feet (½ mile). Here the track leads up a spur of moraine stone for 1,300 feet, and then another spur, about 300 feet, leads to the foot of the main moraine (3 miles). This moraine is about 100 to 200 feet high and is a rugged pile of enormous sharp stones. Crossing this stony barrier the glacier is reached. It is about ¾ mile across and rises 500 to 600 feet. One-third is good going, one-third would have been impassable without ice axes, as we had to cut out every step, and the last third was the worst, as though not quite so steep, the ice was soft and at each step we sank into it a foot or 18 inches. The highest point was estimated at 18,200 feet. The labour of climbing and crossing the glacier at this height was very severe. Men fell again and again. The pass is the top of an almost vertical cliff and the actual ridge an absolute knife edge, being the cleavage edge of rocks set at an angle of about 45°. A very difficult descent of 300 feet brings the track to a small lake, a very wild place surrounded by glaciers and moraines. Yaks can be brought from Momay Samdong to this point. The outlet stream of this lake, Sebu Chu, is followed down the steep side of an ancient moraine till a large lake is reached (6 miles), which takes the streams and moraine from several glaciers. From this for one mile is a difficult bit of track round the toe of an enormous moraine, apparently on the move (7 miles).
				After passing this there is a comparatively easy descent to the valley where the river has to be crossed. About ½ mile on are three hot springs, and another 1½ miles brings the track to Momay Samdong (9 miles), a nice village on a slope (15,587). It contains about 12 stone huts. It is the most northern of the Lachung habitations and is on the road from Chungthang to the Donkhya La. Lots of camping-ground for 2,000 men; good water and grazing; no fuel.
				Owing to the steepness and ruggedness of the pass this road is practically of no use except for a very small number of good climbers. It is absolutely impassable for baggage animals, loaded or unloaded, and could not be rendered practicable. No native will cross unless it is free from snow. The glacier which has to be crossed requires the use of ice axes.
				N.B.—The correct height of the pass is 17,580 feet.

Route No. 32.

FROM TANGU TO SITONG, *viâ* LONGTONG LA AND PHALLUNG LA.

Authority and date.—SURGEON-CAPTAIN A. PEARSE, A.M.S., DECEMBER 1895.

No. of stages.	Names of stages.	DISTANCES.		REMARKS.
		Inter-mediate.	Total.	
				General direction, north-north-west.
1	SITONG . . .	10¼	10¼	The road, which is a bridle path, branches from Route 22 at Tangu village and follows the right bank of the Tangu Chu for 5½ miles. At 300 yards from Tangu a shallow rapid stream, 3 yards broad, is crossed and

Route No. 32—*concld.*

No. of stages.	Names of stages.	Distances.		Remarks.
		Inter-mediate.	Total.	
				the road then ascends a steep spur by zig-zags for ¾ of a mile through rhododendron and fir jungle to an elevation of 13,450 feet. It then rises by easy gradient along the south-eastern slope (which is grassy) of Komuthongu mountain (generally called La Sha by the natives) for 2½ miles keeping an elevation of about 500 feet above the Tangu Chu, two streams being crossed. At 3½ miles there is a steep ascent for 200 yards up a rocky spur, after which the gradient is again easy till the foot of the Longtong La (4½ miles) is reached, whence there is a steep ascent for ¼ of a mile to the top of the pass; elevation 14,865 feet. There is then a slight descent for 300 yards where a stream is crossed, and then a slight and gradual ascent to Dambashi, 5⅝ miles from Tangu and elevation 15,060 feet. From Dambashi there is a steep ascent along a spur in a northerly direction for ¾ of a mile. The gradient is then easy till the top of the Phalung La, elevation 16,150 feet, is reached at 7½ miles from Tangu. The descent from this is steep for 200 yards, but subsequently by easy gradient to within a ¼ of a mile of the Lachen river where it becomes rather steep. The river is crossed at 10 miles from Tangu, to join route 22, a short distance below Sitong. The whole of this road is passable for baggage animals, though in one or two places it is difficult.

Route No. 33.

From TANGU to SEBU LA.

Authority and date.—Surgeon-Captain A. Pearse, A.M.S., December 1895.

No. of stages.	Names of stages.	Distances.		Remarks.
		Inter-mediate.	Total.	
1	Sebu La . . .	7	7	As far as Dambashi, see Route No. 32. From Dambashi the road skirts the western margin of some marshy ground (200—300 yards in breadth) through which the Phalung Chu runs. At 2 miles a shallow stream, 3 yards broad, is crossed. From this point the road is over slightly undulating grass land to the foot of the Sebu La (4½ miles) when it crosses the Phalung Chu to ascend the pass. This ascent is very steep over loose rocks and earth for ¾ of a mile; it then becomes more easy until within 300 feet of the summit when it passes on to a glacier. Laden yaks and ponies are said to be able to cross the pass. (Note.—See, however, General Yeatman-Biggs' remarks on this pass in Route 31.)

Route No. 34.

From TANGU to NAKU LA, *via* LUNGNA LA.

Authority and date.—Lieut. W. F. O'Connor, R.A., September 1896.

No. of stages.	Names of stages.	Distances.		Remarks.
		Inter-mediate.	Total.	
1	Gyepo Nathang . .	6	6	First up the left bank of the Lachen river about one mile. Cross river by a strong wooden bridge and turn sharp to the left up the side of an ancient moraine. Down other side of moraine and up valley due west. Valley flat and marshy for one mile ; then rise gradually to height of 14,000 feet to small flat, 200 yards by 100, called Gyepo Nathang. Large hollow rocks close by give good shelter. Wood and water plentiful. Road bad, rocky, and for some way up bed of stream, but passable for ponies or mules. A little coarse herbage near the camp for grazing animals.
2	Tebli	11	17	Across Lungna La.
				Up a steep ascent of 600 feet to a small lake. Road hence to summit of pass alternately very steep and nearly level, last 300 or 400 feet impassable for ponies or laden mules. Summit of pass, 16,100. Descent from summit very steep down almost perpendicular cliffs. Small lake, 15,000 feet. Hence track down valley very fair due west. Valley debouches on Naku Chu (Lanok Chu of survey map) about ½ mile above Tebli, which is a small flat maidan about 500 yards by 300 yards by the edge of the stream. Just above there is a Tibetan sheep-fold formed by a circular wall, 3 feet high, enclosing a space 10 or 12 yards across. Scrub juniper and yak dung give good fuel. Water from river ; a little grazing for animals. Surrounding hills very bare, parched and stony—not a single tree and only a few stunted bushes lower down. River here averages from 20 to 40 feet in width, and where widest is from 2 to 3 feet deep and easily fordable although the current is strong : bottom stony. There is an easy ford just opposite Tebli. The Lachen people use the Lungna La to bring their yaks into Lhonak during the summer months, but the pass could not be used for either ponies or laden mules. Elevation of Tebli, 14,500. Two hours from Gyepo Nathang to summit of Lungna La : 3½ from Pass to Tebli.
				This pass could be crossed in one day from Tangu, but would be a very severe march for coolies.
3	Naku La . . .	9	26	The valley of the Naku Chu runs north-north-east for about 6 miles for the whole of which distance the rise is only 100 feet, and can be ascended without difficulty on either side of the stream. On the left bank the valley consists of a series of perfectly level grassy maidans, some as much as 800 yards long by 400 yards wide, separated from each other by spurs running down from the hills on the east. On the right bank the hills come steeply down to the stream, but an easy level track runs along the side of the slopes. After 6 miles the stream forks : the main stream flowing north and south for about ½ mile, and another stream joining it from the north-east from some large snow fields and high peaks ; both streams easily fordable. The main stream now rises more rapidly and turns again north-north-east, another small tributary joining it from a gully to the west. After ½ mile of rocky ground the valley opens out into a level maidan about 1,000 yards by 500 yards running nearly due east. The ascent to the pass is at the north-east corner of this, and consists of a steep stone slope about 300 feet high. This could only be climbed by ponies or laden mules with difficulty, and could be strongly defended from above ; but a track for animals could be made up the slopes to the left of the pass which are not very steep and are bare and free from rocks or boulders, and in this way the pass could be turned. Beyond the pass the country consists of an undulating grassy plain falling gently for 3 or 4 miles from the watershed. On the right of the top of the pass is a small triangular lake.

Route No. 34—*concld.*

No. of stages.	Names of stages.	Distances.		Remark .
		Inter-mediate.	Total.	
				The whole of this road (with the exception of the last 300 feet) is easily passable for ponies or laden mules, and the streams are fordable at almost any point. The Tibetans feed great numbers of yaks here during the summer months, leaving the valley for Tibet during the first fortnight in September with great herds, consisting of as many as 500 yaks. Grass is fairly plentiful at the bottom of the valley. Scrub juniper grows right up to the foot of the pass. Height of pass 17,300 feet by aneroid barometer. About ¼ mile north of Tebli on the left bank of the Naku Chu stand the ruins of an old Tibetan blockhouse — 4 walls about 12 or 14 feet high, solidly built of stone, outside measurements 24 feet by 18 feet. The roof has fallen in. This ruin stands on the top of a small spur about 100 feet above the river, and commands the ground for some distance in every direction and could be strongly defended.
				The whole of the district drained by the Naku Chu and Langpo Chu is called Lhonak, meaning "the black south," and is regarded by the Tibetans as their own property; and they very much resent the appearance there of any foreigner. Troops could be camped here in any numbers, but fuel would be a great difficulty as the scanty bushes round about would soon be exhausted, and the roads leading to Lhonak are so bad that supplies could only be brought in slowly by coolies.

Route No. 35.

From TEBLI to CHOTEN NIMA LA.

Authority and date.—Lieut. W. F. O'Connor, R A., September 1896.

No. of stages.	Names of stages.	Distances.		Remarks.
		Inter-mediate.	Total.	
1	Camp on Langpo Chu .	12	12	First cross Naku Chu by a ford opposite to Tebli. Current strong, about 2 feet deep, bottom stony, 12 yards wide. Keep west-south-west, leaving stream on left hand, and cross a small pass between two low hills, about one mile from river. Path slopes gently for ½ mile down shallow stony ravine which then opens out into a large grassy maidan (called the Langpo Thang) about 2 miles in length (from west to east) by one mile in width (north to south). On the north edge of this is some marshy ground (where the natives say that wild fowl assemble in enormous numbers during their annual flights up and down to the plains), but the rest is hard and level and quite bare. Crossing the plain the Langpo Chu is reached, which is somewhat difficult to ford on foot as the water is over 3 feet in depth, and the current strong and bottom stony. From here a track runs up to The La, *vide* Route No. 25. Now turn west and follow the left bank of the Langpo Chu until valley forks right and left, the left-hand stream being the main one. Ford stream, here easily done, and keep along right bank of main stream which here runs in a steep narrow gorge—high ancient moraines, rising to a height of about 300 feet on either side. The road to be taken lies on the top of the moraine and offers no difficulties. After 1 mile this gorge opens out into a level valley averaging about 500 yards across, which runs west-south-west for 7 or 8 miles; the bottom of the valley level and gravelly. Low flat-topped moraines on either side. Scrub-bushes

No. of stages.	Names of stages.	DISTANCES.		REMARKS.
		Intermediate.	Total.	
				of various kinds grow in great abundance forming low thickets here and there, through which are well-marked paths made by the yaks which are driven up the stream to graze. Hares abound in great numbers.
				When the gorge spoken of above opens out, cross the stream again at a place where it widens out and flows in several shallow channels, bottom sandy. The left bank is now followed and after about 7 miles a good camping place is reached at an elevation of 15,700 feet, at a spot where a Tibetan sheep-fold is found, which consists of a circular wall, 3 feet high, enclosing a small space 7 or 8 yards across, and a small stone shed. River is generally unfordable, current strong and 4 or 5 feet deep, bottom stony, but in places it widens and grows shallow and is easily crossed. This valley can be ascended by ponies or laden mules. General direction is west-south-west. Scrub jungle plentiful near camp for fuel. Water from stream. Scanty grass for grazing.
2	CHOTEN NIMA LA	7	19	Follow the left bank of the stream for ½ mile to where small tributary joins from north-north-west. Cross this and turn north-west up steep grassy spur. After a climb of 700 feet a bare plateau is reached which runs alongside the stream some 700 or 800 feet above it and averages 3 or 4 miles in width, being bounded by the snow peaks of the frontier. Change direction north-north-west, and after ½ mile the pass will be seen between 2 snow peaks about 5 miles ahead. It is easily distinguished by 4 or 5 pinnacles of rock about 20 feet in height which stand along the summit of the pass. Approach to bottom of pass offers no difficulties, some bare stony hillocks intervening. Hence to top of pass very difficult; ascent consists of a steep stone slide 700 feet in height; it is almost perpendicular, and cumbered with crumbling *débris* from heights on each side. Quite impassable for ponies or mules, though coolies can get up without any great difficulty. Summit of pass 18,650 by aneroid barometer. From the top of the pass a magnificent view can be obtained into Tibet. The head of the valley of the Langpo Chu is enclosed by a number of very fine snow peaks ranging from 20,000 to 24,000 feet in height, from which glaciers run down almost to the level of the stream. The actual head of the valley is a chaotic mass of glacier and moraine. There is said to be a pass, the Jongsong La, leading out of this valley into Nepal, but I was unable to ascertain whereabouts it lay; from the general configuration of the country, it must be extremely lofty and difficult.
				NOTE.—The Naku Chu runs in a fairly level and open bed for a mile or two below its junction with the Langpo Chu, and no difficulty would be found in making a path fit for animal transport for this distance. Beyond this point, however, the natural difficulties are said to be great, *vide* Route No. 36.
				The distances given here are only approximate and even so very deceptive; from the last camp reported upon to the top of the Choten Nima pass is a good 6 hours' work for coolies. It takes a full hour to ascend the last 300 feet to the summit of the pass.

Route No. 36.

From ZEMU SAMDONG to NAKU LA, *viá* ZEMU CHU.

Authorities and dates.—Political Officer, Sikkim, 1892 and 1894, and Lieut. W. F. O'Connor, R.A., 1896.

No. of stages.	Names of stages.	Distances.		Remarks.
		Intermediate.	Total.	
				Zemu Samdong is situated between Lamteng and Tallum Samdong, *vide* Route No. 22.
				From the bridge the road lies up the left bank of the Zemu river. At present no practicable path exists, but one would have to be cut out of the jungle. After one day's march the junction of the Zemu Chu with the Naku Chu (coming from the north-west) is reached. Here the Naku Chu must be crossed and the road lies up its right bank, crossing the stream again higher up. All this is through thick jungle. The bridges are said to be in repair. At an elevation of about 13,500 feet the jungle ceases, and an open country is reached, the Naku Chu running in a deep gorge with steep hills on either side, until shortly before its junction with the Langpo Chu, when the country becomes more open (*vide* Route No. 35). Above the junction of these two rivers an easy path may be followed in quite open country as far as Tebli, whence to Naku La, see Route No. 34.
				It is said to be 5 days' journey from Zemu Samdong to the Naku La, but at present no road practicable for transport animals or ponies exists, and travellers would have to be prepared to construct their own bridges. The Zemu Chu has its origin in the immense glacier which descends from the northern flanks of Kangchenjunga, and issues from a cavern at its eastern extremity. The surface of the glacier is covered with stones and *débris*, and is enclosed by bare hills on the north and south.

Route No. 37.

From TALUNG to LAMTENG, *viá* TUKCHUM LA.

Authority and date.—Lieut. W. Strong, R.A., 1897.

No. of stages.	Names of stages.	Distances.		Remarks.
		Intermediate.	Total.	
				This path connects Talung monastery (*vide* Route No. 25) with Lamteng village in the Lachen valley. Three marches. The first from Talung to camp just below the pass is very steep, and it is necessary in one place to unload the coolies and drag loads over an overhanging rock with ropes.
				Second march cross the pass, which is fairly easy.
				Third march arrive at Lamteng.

Route No. 38.

FROM BE TO JONGRI, *vid* GUICHA LA.

Authority and dates.—POLITICAL OFFICER, SIKKIM, 1892 AND 1894.

No. of stages.	Names of stages.	DISTANCES.		REMARKS.
		Inter-mediate.	Total.	
				Be is on the road between Gantok and Naku La (*vide* Route No. 25).
				Ten days' journey by an ill-marked and very little used path, quite impracticable for any form of transport except coolies. One or two enormous ravines are crossed and one day's march is over a glacier. The Guicha La, elevation 15,300 feet, is crossed. Jongri is about 17 miles from Guicha La; intermediate camp at Alukthang where there is a yak-herd's hut.
				For Jongri, *vide* Route No. 39.

Route No. 39.

FROM PAMIONCHI TO KANG LA.

Authority and date.—SIKKIM ROUTE BOOK, 1894, AND MR. C. W. DOVER, 1900.

No. of stages.	Names of stages.	DISTANCES.		REMARKS.
		Inter-mediate.	Total.	
1	RATHONG RIVER	6½	6½	Descend for 4 miles to the village of Chongpon (altitude 4,980 feet), and thence to the bed of the Rungbi (3,160 feet), an affluent of the Rathong, flowing in a deep gully with precipitous sides. The Rungbi is spanned by a rough bamboo bridge without hand-rails, length about 20 yards. Hence cross a lofty spur and descend to the Rathong (altitude 3,000 feet), where camp on a gravelly jungle-clad flat some 50 feet above the river. Ponies can be brought to this point, but no further, as the river is unfordable.
2	YOKSUN	12½	19	Ascend to Yoksun, a picturesquely situated hamlet, path steep and rocky for the first mile or two and then alternately steep and flat. Yoksun is a broad and partially paved platform on which stand two temples. Hence a path leads to Dubdi monastery, which is situated at an elevation of 6,520 feet, or nearly 1,000 feet above Yoksun. This path is broad and skilfully constructed, leading up a steep slope covered with forest.
				Alternative Route.
1	KETSUPERRI	...	...	Descend 3,500 feet, leaving Chongpon village on the right and the Mali monastery on the left, and cross the Rungbi river, elevation 3,300 feet; thence cross the Mali spur and descend to the Tengling river, after crossing which ascend to Ketsuperri, passing the village of Tengling *en route*. The Ketsuperri lake is a sheet of water some 300 to 500 yards across in the rains and standing at an elevation of 6,040 feet; it lies in a hollow surrounded on all sides by dense forest. The Ketsuperri temples occupy a spur some 500 feet above the lake.
2	YOKSUN	...	...	Descend to the Rathong river (3,790 feet), which is here a turbulent stream flowing in a bed 12 yards broad, and ascend for 1,800 feet to Yoksun.
3	CAMP	...	...	From Yoksun the route lies for the first mile over the Yoksun flat, and then winds along the almost precipitous east flank of the Rathong through thick forest and about 1,000, feet above the bed of the stream. Numerous streams are crossed, spanned by rough

Route No. 39—*concld.*

No. of stages.	Names of stages.	DISTANCES.		REMARKS.
		Intermediate.	Total.	
				bamboo bridges, and here and there precipices are ascended with the aid of notched poles. Numerous extensive landslips are crossed. Camp at an altitude of 6,676 feet. The waterfalls of Barabesong are passed *en route;* the mountains throughout the march are very precipitous. The camping-ground is called Tubu; a small torrent flows close at hand.
4	BAKIM	...	...	Proceed north-west up the Rathong river, which is here a furious torrent; cross the river by a rough bridge and ascend a steep hill called Mon Lepcha. Encamp at a place called Bakim, a forest of yew, oak, rhododendron and small bamboos, elevation 8,650 feet.
5	MON LEPCHA HILL	...	...	Ascent is continued at times up steep slopes and at others over flat terraces; water is found here and there in pools. Camp on the summit of Mon Lepcha (elevation 13,080), a broad flat fringed by a copse of wild rose, barberry, and rhododendrons. Heather is abundant here, and forms good fuel.
6	JONGRI	...	36	Path leads north-west along an open, rounded, bare mountain covered with enormous boulders of gneiss; the soil is a thick clay in which are numerous depressions, which in the rains form the beds of pools. Jongri consists of two stone huts on the bleak face of a spur, elevation 13,000 feet, and an extensive tract of yak pasture land, situated at the foot of Kabur on a southern spur from that mountain. The spur is broad and undulating, devoid of forest, covered with good grass intermixed with rhododendron scrub. The hill-side contains numerous springs.
7	KANG LA	...	...	Road crosses the Singalela range at an elevation of about 15,000 feet, south of Kabur and north of a mountain which forms a conspicuous feature southwest from Jongri, as a crest of black fringed peaks tipped with snow. The Kang La is 16,740 feet above sea-level.
				NOTE.—This route is impassable even for yaks. The distance from Yoksun to Jongri is about 17 miles.

Route No. 40.

FROM PAMIONCHI TO THE GAMOTHANG LAKE DISTRICT.

Authority and date.—SIKKIM ROUTE BOOK, 1894.

No. of stages.	Names of stages.	DISTANCES.		REMARKS.
		Intermediate.	Total.	
1	TALET	...	...	Follow the Dentam road (*vide* Route No. 41) for one mile past Sangachelling monastery; then take a road to the right which crosses the ridge and descends on the other side to Talet.
2	PHIONG LANG	...	...	Descend to the Rungbi river, and proceed up its course to camp.
3	CHUNJOM	...	...	The course of the Rungbi river is followed throughout this march.
4	YAMPUNG	...	..	Leave the Rungbi on the left, and ascend to Yampung.
5	GAMOTHANG	...	...	Ascend the Tangknin La, cross the ridge, and descend to the Gamothang lakes. From here a path leads to Kabali bazar in Nepal.
				NOTE.—Ponies can traverse this road after snow has melted; there are, however, some difficult places. Yaks are taken up this route to grazing grounds at Jongri.

Route No. 41.

FROM PAMIONCHI TO CHIABHANJAN, *via* DENTAM.

Authority and date.—LIEUT. W. F. O'CONNOR, R.A., 1896.

No. of stages.	Names of stages.	DISTANCES.		REMARKS.
		Inter-mediate.	Total.	
1	DENTAM . . .	10	10	Road from Pamionchi runs along the summit of the ridge through forest for about 2 miles, when the monastery of Sangachelling is reached; it is perched on the summit of the highest point of the ridge at an elevation of 7,040 feet. It is a curious old place, well worth a visit, the grounds around it being laid out with more taste than is usual, with flowers and shrubs. From here a fine view is obtained. The road does not actually pass the monastery, but runs below it skirting the hill upon which it is built. Follow the crest of the ridge for another mile; then road winds down southern face of hill at an easy gradient, forest growing gradually thinner and being replaced by cultivation. Several small streams are crossed. Road is good, and passes numerous farms, mostly Nepalese. Reach the Kulhait Chu opposite Dentam, and cross by strong wooden bridge. Valley open and level on right bank. A short steep ascent to bungalow, for description of which *vide* Route No. 10. Elevation of bungalow, 4,500 feet.
2	CHIABHANJAN . .	8	18	For road from Dentam to Chiabhanjan, *vide* Route No. 10. NOTE.—It will now be seen that a good road exists right across Sikkim from west to east from Chiabhanjan on the Nepal frontier to Pamionchi *via* Dentam, from Pamionchi to Gantok (*vide* Route No. 24), and from Gantok to Gnathong, *via* Lagyap La, *vide* Route No. 14. Elevation of bungalow, 10,320 feet.

Route No. 42.

FROM PAMIONCHI TO NAMPUK, *via* LINGDAMTSO OR DALLING.

Authorities and dates.—SIKKIM ROUTE BOOK, 1894, AND Mr. J. C. WHITE, POLITICAL OFFICER IN SIKKIM, 1897.

No. of stages.	Names of stages.	DISTANCES.		REMARKS.
		Inter-mediate.	Total.	
1	LINGDAMTSO OR DALLING	...	...	For descent to Rangit river, *vide* Route No. 8, Stage 3. Cross the river and after a steep ascent of 2,500 feet up a long spur reach Lingdamtso (elevation 5,330 feet), and camp on a flat piece of ground surrounded by extensive pools of water. *Alternative route to the above between Pamionchi and Lingdamtso.* There is also a northern route between Pamionchi and Lingdamtso, which has been described by Major Judge, R.E., as follows:— *Pamionchi to Tassiding.*—An ascent of about 1,000 feet from Pamionchi village to Pamionchi monastery (elevation 6,840 feet), thence a very steep descent to Sat Yong village (5,475 feet) followed by a more gradual descent to the Rathong river, which is here a breed

Route No. 42—*concld.*

No. of stages.	Names of stages.	Inter-mediate.	Total.	REMARKS.
				and rapid stream, spanned by a bridge, with banks clothed in dense jungle; thence path ascends to a saddle between the Senan and Tassiding monasteries (elevation 4,075 feet), when path turns south and ascends to Tassiding, elevation 4,850 feet, by a narrow ridge. Greater part of the march is through dense forest. Senan monastery is situated to the north of and on the same ridge as the Tassiding monastery, a path connecting the two.
				Tassiding to Lingdamtso.—A steep descent from camp to the Rangit river, which is here unfordable, bed 200 feet wide, channel 50 feet, depth from 6 to 20 feet; banks and bed very rocky. River is spanned by a bamboo bridge 55 feet long and 15 feet above water-level, passable only to infantry. A cane suspension bridge is constructed during the rains a little higher up the stream; baggage animals can be swum across 30 yards below bridge. Road practicable to baggage animals. The river is crossed at an elevation of 2,225 feet, hence a steep ascent to Chosing or Changsa village, 3 houses (5,100 feet), followed by an almost level road to Lingdamtso, where road under report is struck.
2	YANGONG MONASTERY .	...	...	The ground in the immediate vicinity of Lingdamtso is cleared. Path ascends and enters forest at 5,600 feet, and continues rising to the summit of the Rabong La (6,000 feet). This pass is a saddle in the range connecting the Moinam (10,637 feet) and the Timbila (7,892 feet) peaks, both of which are on a range which springs from Kangchenjunga. Descending by a steep and slippery path cross the Rungpo Chu, a fordable stream, flowing down a steep incline at a rapid pace; the stream is 80 feet wide, and has gravelly banks of a loose formation, elevation at crossing 4,225 feet. Ascend to the village of Pading, after which road is level for a bit (elevation 5,400 feet), followed by a slight ascent and a final drop to Yangong, elevation 5,225 feet. Below the Yangong monastery is a lake 100 yards across. Yangong is a village of 10 houses, standing on open and well-watered ground; fair camping-ground.
3	NAMPUK . .	...	...	Descend the spur on which the monastery is situated through forest; a fairly easy descent as far as the village of Gozuri (3,000 feet), after which road drops more steeply, joining Route No. 11 at the junction of the Rungpo with the Teesta at a spot known as Rungpo Thang. NOTE.—The portion of the road between Lingdamtso and the Teesta river is only passable to pack animals with the greatest difficulty.

Route No. 43.

FROM RHENOCK TO LAGYAP LA, *via* DEKKELING.

Authorities and dates.—MAJOR PEARSON, R.A., 1883-84, AND CAPTAINS TRAVERS AND FOULERTON, 1888.

No. of stages.	Names of stages.	Inter-mediate.	Total.	REMARKS.
1	DEKKELING . . .	6	6	Dekkeling is on the Rhenock-Pakyong road, about 2 miles short of Pakyong. For this march, *vide* Route No. 4.

Route No. 43—*concld.*

No. of stages.	Names of stages.	DISTANCES.		REMARKS.
		Inter-mediate.	Total.	
2	GHETHI . . .	7	13	Descend from Dekkeling to the Roro Chu through bamboo jungle with little undergrowth; thence ascend to the summit of a ridge, which is followed; road is here fairly level; houses and patches of cultivation are met with. Latterly forest is entered and a sharp ascent is commenced, which continues for a mile, then becomes more easy. Ascent continues to camp; a small stream, the only water between the Roro Chu and camp, being crossed at 6½ miles. The whole of this march is practicable to animal transport. Camping-ground at Ghethi very small and bad, and water-supply precarious; the water is found in a hollow about 100 yards to the north of the knoll at the west end of the camping-ground; camp would accommodate about 100 men.
3	DEPUK . . .	9	22	March commences with numerous short, sharp ascents, the path being between high steep banks so close together that a cooly with his load can only just pass between them. From 1½ to 2½ miles road is fairly level, after which steep ascents are again encountered; hitherto march is through dense tree forest, which gives place to bamboo at 3½ miles. At 7¾ miles a steep descent at a gradient of ⅓; road being cut into steps; at 8½ miles and on to camp path follows the summit of a ridge, numerous small knolls being climbed. Path throughout through dense jungle, at first tree forest and latterly bamboo, and quite impassable to any arm but infantry. Camp in an exposed situation on the summit of the ridge, space available for 1,500 men if scattered and jungle cleared. Excellent spring of water in a hollow to the north of camp and about 50 yards below it. Darjeeling and Padong are visible from here. Plenty of bamboo forage in vicinity.
4	LAGYAP LA . . .	1	23	The Lagyap La is reached almost immediately on leaving camp, and here the road from Gantok to Gnathong is struck. This road follows the crest of the ridge the whole way, and is generally precipitous and covered with boulders. At Jongchen there is an open space where 500 men could encamp. It is quite impassable for laden mules.
				NOTE.—This route was made use of during the Sikkim Expedition of 1888 as a means of flanking the enemies' position at Lingtu, and at the same time of avoiding the necessity of passing through Gantok, which was at the time undesirable owing to political considerations. The troops detailed for this duty had, however, only proceeded as far as Jongchen when they were recalled. It is unlikely that it will ever again be used.

W. F. O'C.

Route No. 44.

FROM CHIABHANJAN TO JONGRI, *via* GAMOTHANG LAKE DISTRICT.

Authority and dates.—POLITICAL OFFICER OF SIKKIM, 1892 AND 1894.

No. of stages.	Names of stages.	DISTANCES.		REMARKS.
		Inter-mediate.	Total.	
				General direction, north.
				This road is practicable to ponies throughout.
				NOTE.—The road lies north along the crest of the Singale-la ridge and is well-defined and offers no difficulties. There is no water (except one small pond) until the Gamothang Lake District is reached. It is much used by Nepalese shepherds who drive large flocks of sheep up to the higher pastures during the rains. Jongri could be reached in 3 stages from Chiabhanjan.

W. F. O'C.

CHUMBI VALLEY ROUTES.

Route No. C1.

FROM CHUMBI TO PHARI.

Authorities.—CAPTAIN F. C. COLOMB, 42ND GURKHA RIFLES; FROM NATIVE INFORMATION.

No. of stages.	Names of stages.	DISTANCES.		REMARKS.
		Inter-mediate.	Total.	
1	LINGMATHANG SHO	5	5	Cross the Ammo Chu at Chumbi by a wooden bridge after which the road is level up the left bank of the river. At 1 mile there is a second wooden bridge by which a branch road crosses to Eusakha village and thence leads to the Thanka La and on to Lachung in Sikkim. Main road still keeps up the left bank of the river passing, half a mile on, the junction of the Rido Chu and Mo Chu, on the fork of which is Fakchang village, a collection of a few houses and a monastery on flat ground. A mile on is another wooden bridge leading to Tugui, a village of 12 houses, and here a path turns off leading up hill by an easy slope to Gangoo and down again to the river at Shookoteng (Tomaushed?). This road is important as it turns the whole of the fortifications between Gub Jong and Galling. The valley now closes in and half a mile on, on the left bank of the river, is Gupta, a large cave and halting-place, opposite which on the right bank and considerably higher is Gub Jong. Here there is a Chinese defence wall similar to that at Yatung; its length is about 150 yards and it extends between a series of precipitous cliffs on the south-east and the Mo Chu on the north-west. The hills to the east of the wall are so rocky that an outflanking movement on that quarter would be a matter of difficulty; on the right bank of the river, however, the position may be turned by the road to Gangoo noted above. The main road passes through a gateway in the wall and in rear are about 100 houses for the guard and a parade-ground. The garrison is entirely Chinese, the Tibetan officers and soldiers residing on the right bank of the river at Gub Jong.
				Between Gupta and Chotenkerpo—a temple—there are a series of defence walls, which, for half a mile, cross the road at intervals, and behind each wall are the quarters for the guard. At Gupta there is a wooden bridge by which communication is kept up between the right and left bank of the river.
				On the right bank of the river is a rocky spur on the summit of which is Gub Jong. Above the fort the slope is more gentle and half a mile up is the village of Gangoo, 100 houses, and Kerumchi monastery, the ground in the vicinity being level and cultivated. Three miles above Gangoo (north-east?) is a hill called Momenteng whence Phari and Rinchengong are both visible; this hill would form a good signalling station. From Chotenkerpo the valley is still narrow for half a mile to Galling village where it opens out a little. The village contains about 140 houses and is situated on flat, cultivated ground about 150 yards from the bank of the river which is spanned by a wooden bridge just below the village.
				On the right bank of the Mo Chu is a village of about 10 houses called Tomaushed (Shookoteng?) and above this again up the hill-side is Pumugang monastery and 7 villagers' houses.
				Beyond Galling the valley closes in again and is shut in on either hand by precipitous rocky slopes, road narrow and rising gently. Ribunkha, a village of about 40 houses, is passed and 1 mile from Galling the lower end of a large, open grassy plain is reached, called Lingmathang, the southern extremity being designated Lingmathang Sho, and the northern Lingmathang Go. Cross the river by a wooden bridge at

No. of stages.	Names of stages.	Distances.		Remarks.
		Inter-mediate.	Total.	
				the southern end of the plain and camp on the right bank of the river ; space available for a large force. As far as Lingmathang the road has at intervals passed through considerable stretches of pine forest which here gives place to scrub rhododendron and juniper.
2	Kamparab Bridge	9¾	14¾	Road for 1 mile over the open valley to Lingmathang Go, the northern extremity of the flat, then half mile on cross the river to the left bank by a wooden bridge and reach Pangkho, a halting-place ; no village ; this half mile of road is very rough and the valley narrow. The valley is again open and wider for one mile to Tongshong, a halting-place, and continues to be so for another mile to Samsathang. (Thang means valley or flat). A fairly easy ascent of half a mile is now encountered, and Khema Lachung, a low saddle, is crossed ; hence for half a mile the valley is very narrow and the road bad. Cross the river by a wooden bridge to Gautsa, a cattleshed, and 300 yards on the road emerges on Gauthang, an open, flat valley where 600 men could encamp. Here there is a large cave. Road is now very rocky and for the next half mile to Takerpo there are many ascents and descents. Takerpo is a cave and is generally used as a traveller's halting-place. Valley continues narrow and road bad passing Gyimdho, Langbup and Shangnama, all small halting-places, at intervals of about half a mile each, and 1 mile beyond the last of these, road in the same condition as above, is Dotha, a stone rest-house ; no camping-ground available for troops.
				The road now becomes very bad and ascends steeply for a mile to Charang (rang means rocks) over rocks, no village, and half a mile on a tributary stream is crossed by a wooden bridge called Samchen where there is a small camping-ground. Hence valley continues narrow and the road is cut in the face of its precipitous, rocky sides, but is level to Kamparab, a bridge across the Mo Chu. Here there is flat ground sufficient for 2,000 men to encamp.
3	Phari	6½	21¼	Cross the Mo Chu to the left bank, and hence to Phari the road crosses open rolling plains, and offers no difficulties to the advance of troops.
				Half a mile beyond the bridge is Shamagya, a stone rest-house at the foot of a hill, round the base of which the road now winds.
				At 1½ miles on by a level road is Agang, another rest-house, and the same distance on again is Damnama (green flat), a grassy flat.
				One mile beyond this pass Sasi, a grazing station, and after 1½ miles more reach Samdup Lhakang (lhakang means temple), a temple. Hence it is half a mile by a good road over open country to Phari.
				The town stands on a slight elevation, its northern end ascending the hill-side slightly towards Phari Jong ; it contains about 300 mud-walled houses and many shops, where provisions and clothing of all kinds are obtainable. Tobacco, cloth and fruit, which are brought in from Bhutan, are to be had in the *bazar*, and fish are said to be plentiful. Vegetables are scarce, but cattle are very numerous.
				No grain crops ripen in the vicinity, but wheat is grown for fodder and sold in the *bazar* at Rs. 2 per maund. A 10 per cent. tariff on all goods sold goes to the Phari Jongpens.
				Phari Jong is built on a flat-topped hill, ¼ mile north of the town ; it has triple stone walls, and the central building is 5 stories high and roofed with dried mud.
				The above road is used at all seasons of the year by mule caravans.

Route No. C2.

From PHARI to PARO (in Bhutan).

Authorities and date.—Captain F. C. Colomb, 42nd Gurkha Rifles; from native information, 1895.

No. of stages.	Names of stages.	Distances.		Remarks.
		Inter-mediate.	Total.	
1	Kashana . . .	6¼	6¼	This road is greatly used by traders between Phari and Paro. It is passable to laden mules and ponies. For the first 1½ miles the road is level over open grassy country to Thangbi, a camping-ground. At 2½ miles is Chumi Goidang, another camping-ground; here the ascent to the Pempa La commences; at 4½ miles a spur, called Shari Gong, is crossed where ground is available for camping, and at 4¾ miles the Pempa La is reached after an easy ascent. The whole ascent to the pass from Phari is very easy. Towards Bhutan the descent is very steep for the first 300 yards, but is not so bad as to prevent mules regularly crossing the pass. At 6¼ miles, after a steady descent, reach a rest-house called Kashana, at the source of the Paro Chu; the valley here is open and grassy.
2	Dukgya (Domgit) Jong	13½	19¾	Road is now down the left bank of the Paro Chu for 1 mile to Gyensa (Ghassa?), a village of three houses, of which two are occupied all the year round by herds-men. The village is under the jurisdiction of Dukgya (Domgit) Jong. Descending continually along the bank of the stream pass Chakna Chorten, a temple, at 1½ miles, and Shingkharab, a village of 2 houses per-manently occupied, at 3¼ miles. Road is now along a level valley up to 6½ miles when Shanana (Sana?), a village of 6 houses, is reached; here a Tungpa resides who is responsible to the Bhutanese Government for the collection of rents and taxes. These dues are paid in salt which is forwarded to Paro, the amount so realised amounting to about 15 maunds per month. In the vicinity of the village wheat, potatoes, and vegetables are grown. The road now crosses to the right bank of the Paro Chu by a wooden bridge, at either end of which are doors which are locked at night. On this bridge is built the residence of the Tungpa or tax-collector. The Paro Chu is only fordable during the winter months. Road again descends, still following the bank of the stream, and passes Chuyu, a village of 4 houses inha-bited by cultivators, at 8¼ miles, and Misi, a village of 8 houses, at 10¼; valley on either side of the stream is flattish and open. Cross the Paro Chu again ¾ mile below Misi by a wooden bridge and at 11½ miles reach Romji, a temple and one house. At 12½ miles pass Chunji, 9 houses, and at 13½ reach Dukgya (Domgit) Jong. Dukgya Jong is situated on the right bank of the river, the village consisting of about 30 houses. The Jong or fort occupies a spur, ¼ mile distant from and above the Paro Chu, and between the river and the fort, the ground is rocky and precipitous. A Jongpen has his residence in the Jong. In the vicinity of the village are extensive stretches of cultivation where troops could encamp. Patches of pine forest occur between Shanana and Dukgya Jong.
3	Paro	5	24¾	Pine forest is now entered, and there is a very steep descent for ¾ mile to the foot of the spur on which the Jong is situated. Here Sinchang, a village of 3 houses, is reached. Hence the road is level for a short distance to Gujo Lungchuk, a wooden bridge, by

No. of stages.	Names of stages.	DISTANCES.		REMARKS.
		Inter-mediate.	Total.	
				which the river is crossed to Nyamgyi, a village of 25 houses, in a large, open valley, closely cultivated with rice and wheat. At one mile, the road still continuing level, pass Chenshi, a village of 25 wooden houses, resembling those in the Chumbi valley, and at 1½ miles, road as before, reach Noimoi, 15 houses; this village is the limit of the Dukgya Jong jurisdiction. Road still continuing level, pass Chendona, 10 houses, at 2 miles and Gyagathang, 40 houses, in an open, flat valley at 2½ miles; here there are ponies, mules, and cattle in large numbers.
				Hence the road is over an open, level valley passing Kyechu Lhakang, a temple and 8 houses, at 3½ miles, and Nemabue, a village of 60 houses, at 4 miles. One mile beyond this, at 5 miles, is Paro, to reach which cross the Paro Chu to the left bank by a good wooden bridge, the roadway of which is roofed over while at either end are gates, tenanted by the bridge guard. On the right bank of the river close to the bridge is a *bazar* on flat ground. To Paro Jong is a very steep ascent of ¼ mile, elevation 7,740 feet; the Jong is surrounded by stone walls, painted white with a broad red bar along the centre horizontally; collected round the Jong there are about 25 houses. The hill-sides about Paro are thickly clothed with pine forest.

Route No. C3.

FROM CHUMBI TO PARO (IN BHUTAN).

Authority and date.—REPORT ON THE EXPLORATIONS OF EXPLORER P. A, 1885-86, PREPARED IN THE OFFICE OF THE TRIGONOMETRICAL BRANCH SURVEY OF INDIA.

No. of stages.	Names of stages.	DISTANCES.		REMARKS.
		Inter-mediate.	Total.	
1	LANGMARPO . . .	12	12	From Chumbi the road runs first down the right bank of the Ammo Chu as far as Rinchengong (for this portion of the road see Route No. 12, stage 3, of the Sikkim routes). Here cross the river by a wooden bridge 100 feet long, and travel south-east along the left bank of the river about 6 miles to opposite the village of Assam Thang. Three miles further on the junction of the Langmarpo Chu with the Ammo Chu is reached. Here there is a small cave which serves as a shelter.
2	Rest-house up valley of LAGULUNG CHU . .	7(?)	19(?)	Continue along left bank of Ammo Chu to junction of Lagulung Chu or Langmar Poohu with main stream. Path now lies up right bank of Lagulung Chu. From junction of Lagulung Chu with Ammo Chu to the Chu La is a distance of about 10 or 12 miles. A short distance below the pass is a *dok* or cattleshed, consisting of 3 houses, where numerous cattle are kept and butter and cheese prepared. The herdsmen are inhabitants of the Ha Chu valley in Bhutan. Soon afterwards a rest-house is reached.

Route No. C3—*concld.*

No. of stages.	Names of stages.	DISTANCES.		REMARKS.
		Inter-mediate.	Total.	
3	DAMTHANG . . .	10(?)	29(?)	ross the Chu La, a pass situated on a lofty spur from the main ridge running down from Masongchung-dung. A small tarn lies to the east of the pass. Continue eastwards for 4 miles to the summit of the Miru La, which is situated on the boundary between the Chumbi valley and Bhutan. Cross the pass and descend in a south-eastern direction for 3 miles to a rest-house called Damthang.
4	GECHUKHA . . .	10(?)	39(?)	Descend along a small stream, the Damthang Chu, to its junction with the Ha Chu, where the valley is half a mile wide, still continue to descend, now along the right bank of the Ha Chu, to the large village of Gechukha, which consists of 20 houses and a monastery.
5	TUMPHIONG JONG . .	(?)	(?)	To opposite Tumphiong Jong from Gechukha is half a day's journey. The Ha Chu is crossed by a large bridge and the road runs down the left bank of the stream. There is also a road down the right bank to Tumphiong Jong. The valley is covered with villages and there is game in abundance.
6	PARO	(?)	(?)	Hence to Paro the road runs north-east crossing a pass called the Chu La, elevation 12,492 feet.
				NOTE.—From the map (sheet No. 7 N.-E. trans-frontier) the distance from Gechukha to Tumphiong Jong would appear to be about 4 or 5 miles ; and from Tumphiong Jong to Paro about 9 or 10.

Route No. C4.

FROM CHUMBI TO LACHUNG, *via* THANKA LA.

Authorities and dates.—CAPTAIN F. C. COLOMB, 4, 2ND GURKHA RIFLES ; FROM NATIVE INFORMATION, 1895.

No. of stages.	Names of stages.	DISTANCES.		REMARKS.
		Inter-mediate.	Total.	
1	THANKA . . .	?	?	Follow the road from Chumbi to Phari (*vide* Route No. 1) for 1 mile crossing to the right bank of the Ammo Chu at Eusakha. A mile beyond Eusakha pass Changra, a cultivation clearing ; here the Rido Chu flows into the Ammo Chu.
				Path now is up the right bank of the Rido Chu through fir forest. At Kobup, a cattleshed, fir forest ceases, and the valley broadens out and is open.
				Road now ascends steadily to Thanka, a pasture ground below the Thanka La, where camp.
2	MEMPHU . . .	?	?	Ascend steeply to summit of the Thanka La and descend to Memphu, a camp on the Sikkim side of the frontier.
				Hence see route 26 of Routes in Sikkim.

Route No. C5.

From PHARI to GHORA LA, *via* KHOMBU.

Authorities and dates.—Surgeon-Captain A. Pearse, A.M.S., 1896 and native information.

No. of stages.	Names of stages.	Inter-mediate.	Total.	Remarks.
1	Samchen . . .	9	9	From Phari proceed south along the Chumbi road as far as Samchen, 9 miles. For this stage, *vide* Route No. C1, stages 2 and 3.
2	Khombu . . .	12 (?)	21 (?)	From Samchen turn North-West up the hill-side, leaving the main road. A path leads to Khombu distant about 12 miles.
3	Ghora La . . .	9 (?)	30 (?)	From Khombu to Khombu Jong is a rise of about 1,900 feet, distance 1½ miles. Khombu Jong is a large square building, partly stone, partly wood, which forms the fort or guard-house for Khombu. Hence ascend by an easy gradient for one mile to Sennacup Chu. From here path is fairly level for two miles. The road now runs along the left bank of the Khombu Chu rising at an easy gradient for two miles. The ascent is now steep over rough rocky ground along the left bank of the Tzozotang Chu for two miles, whence half a mile rise very steep over glacier leads to the summit of the Ghora La, elevation 17,900 feet (?).
				For the descent into Sikkim, see Sikkim Route No. 28.
				The country round about Khombu is described as open and suitable for camping. The natives say that a guard is stationed at Khombu Jong when the Kazi of the district is at Khombu.
				There is said to be a path leading direct to Phari from the junction of the Khombu Chu and Tzozotang Chu.

TIBETAN ROUTES.

Route No. T1.

From PHARI to LHASA, *via* GYANGTSE.

Authorities and dates.—Reports of Great Trigonometrical Survey, 1876, 1879, and 1880, and Turner, 1783.

No. of stages.	Names of stages.	Inter-mediate.	Total.	Remarks.
1	Thuna . . .	17	17	Rise of 2 miles to village of Chu-Gya. Hence gentle ascent to summit of Tang La (very easy) at head of Mo Chu valley (6 miles). Then level to Thuna, 11 miles.
2	Chalu . . .	22	39	Level plain for 19 miles to Ram Tso (lake), lying on east of road; the road then crosses a rivulet which runs into a larger lake further north (named the Kala Tso) by a small bridge built on 2 stone piers. Chalu 3 miles further on. Water from stream.
3	Salu	16	55	From Chalu the road runs along the bank of the stream for 5 miles to the village of Kalapanga on the shores of the Kala Tso. Hence 2 miles along the shore of the lake. After 4 miles the large village of Pika is reached, hence to Salu, 5 miles, the road lying over an extensive plain quite destitute of verdure and covered with small stones. About Kalapanga village

Route No, T1—*contd.*

No. of stages.	Names of stages.	Distances.		Remarks.
		Inter-mediate.	Total.	
				there is extensive cultivation, irrigated by small hill-streams. Salu is a village of 50 houses with some cultivation round it. Water from stream.
4	Changra · · ·	23	78	From Salu the road runs level for 11 miles to Kangma, bordered by low, rounded, sterile hills. From Kangma the main trade route to Lhasa turns off (see below—alternative route). One and a half miles beyond Kangma a hot spring is passed ; hence the road runs almost due north along the river, which further on has a considerable fall and is very rapid, and the roadway is cumbered with stones which fall from cliffs on either side. Where the valley is open there is a considerable amount of cultivation on both sides of the stream. Twelve miles from Kangma Changra is reached, where a stream, the Niru Chu, joins the stream hitherto followed.
5	Gyangtse · · ·	11	89	Some miles from Gyangtse the country opens out and appears more populous and better cultivated. Several villages are passed.
				Gyangtse is a large and important town with a thriving trade. The monastery near by contains 600 monks. There are 2 bridges over the river which in summer is navigated by hide boats. In the centre of the town is a fort which contains 50 Chinese and 200 Tibetan soldiers. Fine crops are raised here, and wheat, barley, radishes, peas, etc., can be procured in the market, also flour, oil, and ghi. Woollen cloth is manufactured in the city.
6	Gabzi · · ·	18	107	The road lies first for a short distance back, up the stream hitherto followed parallel to it a short distance away: then the Penam river is reached and the road follows its right bank. At 6½ and 10½ miles the villages of Thagni and Kotang are passed. At 14 miles the stream is crossed by a bridge. The village of Malang is passed at 16 miles. The road is described as being smooth, wide, and level. At Gabzi there is a "Gyakhang" or Chinese rest-house. Water from stream.
7	Ralung · · ·	18	125	A village on the left bank of the Penam or Penanang river, which now becomes a mere stream. Road from last station level. At ¾ mile stream from the south-east is passed. A road from this point runs alongside this stream, coming from Bhutan. At 1 mile the Penanang is crossed, and the road runs along the river bank. Sakia monastery is passed at 1¼ miles, Gorch village at 2½, and Shelot at 5¾ miles. At 6 miles a stream from the north is crossed, and at 6½ the village of Lungmai is passed, and a stream on which it stands is crossed. Just before reaching Ralung the Penanang Chu is again crossed by a bridge. A small stream is also crossed at Ralung, coming from east and falling into Penanang Chu.
8	Zara · · · ·	17	142	A Chinese post stage. Road from last station at first level and along left bank of Penanang Chu. At 6¼ miles the village of Gomthang stands on the other bank of the stream at the foot of a very lofty snowy mountain. Soon after this the ascent of the Kharo La is commenced by a slight ascent. The summit of the pass is reached at 10 miles. Alongside this point lies an immense glacier. Here the Penanang Chu has its source.
				The descent of the mountain soon commences, and Zara is near the foot. The last part of the road is along the left bank of a small stream rising at the foot of Kharo La mountain.
9	Nangarche Jong ·	14	156	A village on the Yamdok Tso with a Tarjum or resting place and a fort on a small hill. The breadth of the Yamdok Tso varies from 2 to 3 miles, and it is said to be very deep. In the centre of the lake stands a hill, at the foot of which are a number

Route No. T1—*contd.*

No. of stages.	Names of stages.	DISTANCES.		REMARKS.
		Inter-mediate.	Total.	
				of villages. The circumference of the lake is about 45 miles; it is crossed in wicker boats covered with leather. Road from last station level and along left bank of above mentioned stream. A stream from the north is crossed at 2¼ miles, Nigro village passed at 7½ miles, and another small stream crossed at 9½ miles.
10	PETE JONG OR PIAHTE JONG.	15	171	A village with a resting place and a fort on the banks of the Yamdok Tso. The lake from this point stretches to south-east about 20 miles, and then turns west. Road from last station level and along west side of lake. A village is passed at 1 mile (name not known).
				At 4 miles the lake bends in considerably and forms an immense bay. The village of Yasi, at 11 miles, is at the head of this bay, and here the direct road from Shigatse joins the road under report (*vide* route No. 4). Here 4 miles to Pete Jong.
11	KAMBA BARJI .	17	188	Road level along bank of lake as far as Demalung, 11 miles. Here the road leaves the lake and the Kamba La (14,950 feet) is crossed after an ascent of ¾ mile. This pass is on the boundary between the provinces of U and Tsang. From here to Kamba-Barji is about 5 miles. Kamba Barji lies on the south bank of the Brahmaputra.
12	CHUSHUL JONG .	13	201	The road runs north-east along the right bank of the river to Chaksamchori, where the iron chain bridge crosses the river. The bridge is described as follows: it is composed of 4 iron chains, 2 on each side, which are stretched between 2 brick piers, and secured to bollards of wood built into the piers. The distance between the piers is 300 feet. The chains are made of loops each 1 foot in length. From the chains hang suspenders of rope on which the footway is placed. Only one person can cross at a time: but the people are chary of using the bridge at all owing to its insecure condition: they prefer to use the boats belonging to the ferry close by, which are large enough to transport animals across the river, and one large boat will take 30 men at a time. During the rains the bridge cannot be used as its northern end is then separated from the shore by a wide stretch of water.
				From here a road runs south-east along the right bank of the big river.
				The road to Chushul Jong crosses the river here, and runs along the left bank. At 13 miles Chushul Jong is reached.
13	NATHANG . . .	18	219	Level road to Chabonang, a village on the right bank of the Ki Chu or Lhasa river. At ½ mile a stream is crossed coming from north-west which flows into Lhasa Ki Chu 2 miles further down. The road soon reaches the right bank of that river and proceeds along it. Road on to Nathang level. Zame and Janglot villages are passed at 10½ and 11½ miles. At 13 miles road becomes precipitous overhanging the river.
14	LHASA	14	233	Road level along right bank of Ki Chu. Gnang village passed at 6½ miles and at 7¼ Tilung village on the left bank of the Tilung Chu, which is crossed by a stone bridge of 2 arches.
				At 11¼ miles road passes within ¼ mile of Debang monastery, said to contain 7,700 monks.

Alternative Routes.

The main trade route to Lhasa from Phari does not pass through Gyangtse, but runs across from Kangma (*vide* Stage No. 4) to Ralung (*vide* stage No. 7), a distance of about 30 miles, which, however, not having been explored, cannot be reported on. By following

Route No. T1—*concld.*

No. of stages.	Names of stages.	DISTANCES.		REMARKS.
		Inter-mediate.	Total.	
				this route, 2 stages and about 30 miles would be saved, making the journey from Phari to Lhasa, a distance of 203 miles, to be performed in 12 stages. All distances given here must, however, be taken as only approximate, as the various authorities consulted differ considerably. The stages, too, are in all probability much longer than would be undertaken by any troops except cavalry, and intermediate camping-grounds would no doubt have to be selected. Those given here lie at the few scattered villages which are found in this bleak and inhospitable country. The same remarks apply also to the routes which follow.

Route No. T2.

From DONKHYA LA to SHIGATSE, *vid* GYANGTSE.

Authority and date.—REPORTS OF GREAT TRIGONOMETRICAL SURVEY, 1883.

No. of stages	Names of stages.	DISTANCES.		REMARKS.
		Inter-mediate.	Total.	
1	TAG-MAR-KHOB	3	3	Steep descent from summit of Donkhya La (18,100 feet) for more than a mile to a sloping plain called Tso-jynng-thang where travellers usually rest. Tag-mar-khob, 2 miles further on, is a cave. A short march would be necessary as the stage would probably be from Momay Samdong on the Sikkim side, 12 miles from summit of pass. Camp near a stream which feeds the Cholamo lakes.
2	THA-TSHANG	15	18	Road gradually improves after descent from pass, and runs over an elevated gravelly plateau to the Gompa of Tha-Tshang. A stream which runs past a monastery close by is the head waters of the Arun river. From here to Kamba Jong is 22 miles.
3	LA-NGOI (DOK)	23	41	Level road for 11 miles up the Arun, passing several "doks" or herdsmen's camps. Then ascend the La-Ngoi La (16,000 feet), a difficult pass on the north but easy on the south. Two and a half miles down the pass reach La-Ngoi Dok.
4	CAMP	20	61	Three easy passes to be crossed on this march, the Lamo La, Keser La, and Selung La. Between these passes are open level plains with a certain amount of marsh land and many "doks" belonging to Tong-sher Jong which is visible from Selung La. The day's march is continued through open gravelly plains, passing several doks and a few stone-built houses here and there. This route is much used by traders going to the market at Lar.
5	PONG-GONG (DOK)	20	81	Cross the Lama La, a precipitous and rocky mountain pass, 16,800 feet. At the foot of it and the north side is the She-kar monastery. Ten miles further on there is a rock-cut cave at Kyil Khor Ta Dab (Kingatak-dup). The road goes over open gravel-covered plains with occasional fields of barley cultivation, past the village of Kab-shi, near to which the head of the Chi Chu river is crossed; hence to Pong-gong-dok at the western foot of the Pong-gong La.
6	GYANGTSE	12	93	Cross the Pong-gong La (16,200 feet) after a steep and difficult ascent. From the summit a fine view can be had of Gyangtse and neighbourhood. Descend to town of Gyangtse over gravelly plains. To reach monastery cross the Nyang or Paina Chu by a stone bridge, 300 paces long (?) and then pass through ½ mile of gardens.

Route No. T2—*concld.*

No. of stages.	Names of stages.	DISTANCES.		REMARKS.
		Inter-mediate.	Total.	
7	PESHI	16	109	Road lies down the river through a succession of villages surrounded by barley fields. Right and left are stupendous mountain chains. A "2-legged temple" at Peshi.
8	PENAM JONG . .	14	123	Road as before until opposite to Penam Jong where willow gardens and thick woods are found by the river. Jong, resting place and village on right bank of river which is here bridged.
9	SHIGATSE . . .	22	145	As Shigatse is approached villages and cultivation become more frequent, and the country consists of plains and widely extended fields well watered by the Nyang Chu. Frequent streams flowing into the river are crossed. The great monastery of Tashi Lhunpo is passed before arrival at Shigatse. Here there is a great daily market, which occupies the whole street between the monastery and the town. There are 3,000 monks in the monastery. The Nyang Chu flows into the Brahmaputra, 3 miles north of Shigatse.

Route No. T3.

FROM GIAOGONG TO SHIGATSE, *via* KAMBA JONG.

Authority and date.—REPORTS OF GREAT TRIGONOMETRICAL SURVEY, 1875.

No. of stages.	Names of stages.	DISTANCES.		REMARKS.
		Inter-mediate.	Total.	
1	KAMBA JONG . .	17	17	From Giaogong to the Kongra La, see Tibetan Route No. 7. From here gentle descent (7°) for 1½ miles. Hence 7 miles across plain to Kamba Jong. The fort is circular, about 1,500 paces round, and is built on the top of a small mound; the walls, 6 feet thick, are built of uncemented stones.
2	GUMA	21	38	Lungdung village is reached at 5 miles. Hence road to Guma lies over an extensive plain. At 20 miles a road coming from the west from Singsohulung joins road under report. This place is 6 marches distant, and is much used by Nepalese trading with Shigatse.
3	BHADUR . . .	25	63	Fifteen miles from Guma the road ascends a moderate slope for ½ mile to the summit of a pass called the Lasum La. From this pass 7 miles of slight descent leads to the Bhadur plain covered with villages and cultivation. Bhadur consists of 14 groups of houses, 3 to the east of the road and 11 to the west; each group contains about 30 houses. Through the middle of the valley a small stream flows gently to the west; the fields are irrigated and manured; the crops are principally peas and barley.
4	RABGIALING . .	25	88	Six miles beyond Bhadur is a monastery containing 500 lamas. Nine miles further on is a slight ascent to the pass called the Gampo La, where the road crosses a range of hills with peaks about 1,000 feet above the level of the surrounding country; the descent on the other side is a mile and a half long, steep and stony. At the village of Rabgialing, 10 miles from the pass, there is a plantation of dwarf willow trees.
5	SHIGATSE . . .	13	101	From Rabgialing the road passes the large villages of Lugri and Lachung, and meets the road from Ladakh at the south-east corner of the outer wall of the great Tashi Lhunpo monastery.

Route No. T4.

From SHIGATSE to LHASA by the River Road.

Authority and date.—Reports of Great Trigonometrical Survey, 1875.

No. of stages.	Names of stages.	Distances.		Remarks.
		Intermediate.	Total.	
1	NIMO	25	25	Three and a half miles from Shigatse is the enclosed garden of Kumkvaling, 600 paces by 300, with a small Lamasery situated in its midst; near the garden is a bridge over the Paina Chu river, which is 80 paces in length, and constructed of large wooden beams resting on four large piers built of uncemented stones; the bridge is 4 paces wide, and has no hand rails. The banks of the river are moderately steep, the current gentle, and the water alive with large fish; during floods the river is said to rise 12 feet above the ordinary level. Cross to right bank of Paina Chu and follow stream for 2½ miles to its junction with the great river of Tibet, called the Dugshum, above the junction, and the Ekyap Tsangpo, below. It flows in some places in several channels, and in others spreads out into a great expanse of water with scarcely any perceptible current. On the left or north bank many villages are seen, and a plain, varying from 3 to 5 miles in breadth, stretches from the river to a range of rounded hills, which rise to a height of about 1,000 feet above the surrounding country. The river is said never to freeze entirely. Floods occasionally occur. The houses near the river have the lower 3 feet of their walls built of stone, while the upper portion is of unburnt brick; they are low with sloping roofs covered with earth. Some of the houses cover a large area, and contain many little rooms.
2	JAGSA	25	50	Road along right bank of river. There is a regularly organized goods and passenger traffic by boat down stream from Shigatse to Jagsa, divided into two stages at Nimo. The boats are oblong in shape, flat-bottomed, and formed of leather stretched over a wooden framework. A range of snow-clad hills closes in on the right bank of the Tsangpo, about 3 miles to the east of Jagsa, and there is said to be no road along this bank, the river here entering the hills and falling over many rapids. There is no boat traffic between Jagsa and the iron chain bridge over the river at Chaksamchori.
3	CHUCHEN	18	68	From Jagsa the road turns south-east and enters the district of Rung Chung; 5 miles from Jagsa is the village of Jamchen and a monastery of 1,500 monks. The plain about Jamchen is studded with small villages. Beyond Jamchen is the monastery of Humidolma containing 900 monks; from here the road runs through a fertile valley containing several villages, and at 18 miles is the village of Chuchen built on a mound, from the base of which issues a small stream of hot water. Temperature of water 152° F.
4	YASI	26	94	From Chuchen the road passes several villages, two small monasteries, a lake 400 yards × 200, and at 26 miles joins the road from Gyangtse to Lhasa at the village of Yasi on the margin of the Yamdok Tso (see Route No. 1). The range of sand-covered hills overlooking the village of Jagsa on the east continues parallel to the road to the Yamdok Tso, diminishing in height as it gets further east. To the south of the road lie plains bounded by low hills, which in places are close to the road and in places 4 or 5 miles distant. Between Shigatse and Yasi there is considerable traffic.
5	LHASA	64	158	For road from Yasi to Lhasa, see Route No. 1. Alternative route *via* Gyangtse, for which see Routes Nos. 1 and 2. Distance 186 miles.

Route No. T5.

From CHOTEN NIMA LA to GIAOGONG, *vid* VALLEY of YARU CHU in TIBET and KONGRA LA.

Authority and date.—LIEUTENANT W. F. O'CONNOR, R.A., SEPTEMBER 1896.

No. of stages.	Names of stages.	Distances.		Remarks.
		Intermediate.	Total.	
1	CAMP ON TANG LUNG CHU NEAR CHOTEN NIMA MONASTERY.	9	9	From the summit of the Choten Nima pass the descent into Tibet is very difficult. First due north over an easy glacier for ½ mile; then the only way down the valley is between 2 glaciers over a series of ice hummocks thinly covered with shingle which slips under one's feet at every step. After ½ mile of this a small lake is reached, and the glacier stops (elevation 18,000). After this the road offers no particular difficulties, but the descent is steep till from 17,000 feet (where a tributary stream joins from south-west) the valley runs almost level for 8 or 10 miles, when the stream debouches into the plain of the Yaru Chu. On either side of the stream are flat-topped moraines and beyond them a bare rolling country, sloping gradually from the snow peaks of the frontier to the great plain of the Yaru Chu to the north. The stream is easily fordable at any place, and there is plenty of scrub for fuel by the banks. The hills are absolutely bare, except for a little grass lower down, after an elevation of 16,000 feet.
				Camp may be pitched by the bed of the stream near the Choten Nima monastery, which is a place of great sanctity, constantly visited by pilgrims from all parts of Tibet, and the only inhabitant of which for most of the year is an old blind lama. It consists of 2 flat-roofed, square, stone buildings about 20 feet high and 24 feet square, surrounded by a number of smaller outbuildings. It could be strongly defended against an attack from the north and west, but is commanded by a flat-topped moraine in rear. During the summer months large numbers of yaks and sheep are brought up this valley to graze, but by the end of August they are all taken down into the plain below.
				There is great abundance of game here—burrhel, goa and hares, all very tame, as they are never molested by the Tibetans owing to the great sanctity of the neighbourhood. From the surrounding hills fine views may be obtained of this part of Tibet. The country is absolutely bare and of a general red colour. The spurs from the frontier slope down to the plain below in long unbroken slopes, bare of rocks or bushes, and looking as if they had been planed off. The Yaru Chu is seen below winding away to the west as far as the eye can reach; it is said then to turn south, forcing its way through the mountains of the Nepal frontier, and is afterwards known as the Arun and lower down as the Kosi river. In the plain which it waters are several important towns—Tinki Jong, Kamba Jong, Geru, and Tang Lung being the chief ones. In the middle of the plain some small conical hills rise, beyond which a glimpse may be had of the Tsomo Tel Thung Lake. Beyond this plain the whole country consists of low hills, the tops of which are seen to stretch away to the north bounded by the snow peaks of the Central Himalayan chain. Looking westward the snows of the Nepal frontier are seen, peak beyond peak, for many miles. The atmosphere is extraordinarily clear, and distant objects stand out very plainly.
2	CAMP MARKED (1) IN MAP	9	18	From Choten Nima monastery turn east-north-east and travel along the slope of the hills crossing one or two small streams *en route*. This part of the country presents no features of interest, as the spurs are absolutely bare and smooth running down in an unbroken slope to the valley below. There is a little grass up the beds of the streams, where the yaks are brought to graze, and very large herds of these animals may be seen from time to time in the plain below. Flocks

Route No. T5—*concld.*

No. of stages.	Names of stages.	DISTANCES.		REMARKS.
		Intermediate.	Total.	
				of burrhel and goa are frequent on this part of the mountains. The frontier line is an impassable wall of snow and glacier.
				The camping place is in the bed of a stream, where there is a little scrub for use as fuel.
3	CAMP MARKED (2) IN MAP	15	33	Still continue in same general direction over a similar country, gently undulating, until the camping place is reached at an elevation of 15,350 feet, where there are some circular stone walls constituting a sheep-fold, and where during the summer enormous flocks of sheep are fed—3,000 or 4,000 sheep in a flock. There is a stream of good water here and abundance of game. Some of these shepherds are detailed by the Kamba Jong officials to watch the passes along the frontier, and to give instant information in case of any stranger crossing.
4	GIAOGONG . . .	16	49	Continue east-north-east for 2 miles gradually rising on to the top of a long spur, when direction is changed to the south-east and the track rises gradually to the top of an easy pass (16,300 feet), after which the country is undulating for another 2 miles and another small pass (the Sebu La or Sebubu La) is crossed (16,400 feet). Soon after this a long, level plain is reached, at the end of which a third small pass (the Kongra La or Kongra Lama La) is marked by heaps of stones and flags. This pass appears to be on the proper watershed between Sikkim and Tibet, as a small stream flows from the summit into the Gyamtso Nang lake, and hence into the Lachen near Giaogong. From here the road descends to the banks of a lake (the Gyamtso Nang), round the right side of which it runs and then turns south and south-west over an undulating country until Giaogong is reached. The total distance is about 16 miles, and is an easy road for ponies or laden animals. The ground is stony and bare with very little pasturage and no trees or bushes. From the top of the Sebu La all the country in the neighbourhood of Kamba Jong can be plainly seen. The Yaru Chu still runs in a large level maidan bounded by low bare hills to the north.
				The road to Kamba Jong branches off to the north-east about a mile south of the Sebu Pass, crossing a small pass in some low hills close to the road.
				The following information is derived from natives:—
				At Tinki Jong there are 150 soldiers and 30 or 40 other inhabitants.
				Tang Lung is a large town (for this part of Tibet) consisting of 40 or 50 stone houses, and inhabited chiefly by herdsmen.
				At Geru (or Giri) there is a fort with 25 Chinese soldiers.
				At Kamba Jong there are 50 soldiers and 15 or 20 inhabitants besides.
				Dob Ta consists of some 20 houses, and is the property of the Raja of Sikkim. It lies to the north of the Tsomo Tel Thung lake.

N.B.—The distances given here are approximate and the elevations were taken by aneroid barometer.

NOTICE.

1. Europeans visiting Sikkim are required to carry a pass, and, unless provided with a pass, will not be allowed beyond the Darjeeling frontier.

2. The Deputy Commissioner of Darjeeling is authorized to issue passes for the ordinary routes in Sikkim on which bungalows are situated, in accordance with the rules laid down regarding travellers' bungalows in Darjeeling and Sikkim.

The Political Officer in Sikkim (head-quarters at Gantok) is authorized to issue passes to persons wishing to leave the ordinary bungalow routes in Sikkim or to visit Yatung.

Travellers' Bungalows in Darjeeling District and Sikkim.

The following bungalows are now open, besides dâk bungalows at Karseong, Pankabari, and Siliguri:—

Passes issued by the Deputy Commissioner.

Number.	Place.	Distance in miles from Darjeeling.	Distance in miles to next bungalow.	Height in feet above sea-level.
1	Senchal	6	...	
2	Rangaroon	6½	...	8,000
3	Badamtam	7⅔	...	5,700
4	Mirig	25	14 (From Jorepokri)	2,500
5	Kalimpong	28 (*Viâ* Rungit)	10 (From Teesta Bridge)	5,000
		32 (*Viâ* Pashoke)		4,000
6	Rissisum	38 (*Viâ* Rungit)	12 (From Kalimpong)	6,410
7	Jorepokri	13	...	7,400
8	Tanglu	23	9	10,074
9	Sandakphu	38	15	11,929
10	Phalut	51	13	11,811
11	Chiabhanjan	57½	6½	10,320
12	Dentam	64 (50 *Viâ* Chakung)	10	4,500
13	Pamiongchi	76 (42 Direct)	12	6,920
14*	Singlip	38 Direct	4	2,300
15	Rinchingpong	86 (32 Direct)	6	5,000
16	Chakung	98 (20 Direct)	12	5,100
17	Rhenock	48	5	3,000
18	Ari	51 (*Viâ* Pedong)	8 (From Pedong)	4,500
19	Sedonchen	59 or 62	12	6,500
20	Gnatong	69 or 72	9	12,300
21	Namchi	32	15 (From Namchi)	1,200
22*	Tokul	17	21 (From Chakung)	5,200
23	Sang	37	20 (15 miles to Gantok)	4,500
24	Pakyang	53	16 (15 from Pedong)	4,700
25	Gantok	65	12	5,700
26	Tumlong	81	16	6,300
27	Samatek	97	16	6,800
28	Toong	110	13	4,900
29	Cheongtang	122	25	5,100

Under the Deputy Commissioner and Political Officer, Sikkim.

Passes issued by the Executive Engineer, P. W. D., Darjeeling.

Number.	Place.	Distance in miles from Darjeeling.	Distance in miles to next bungalow.	Height in feet above sea-level.
30	Pedong	43	12 From Kalimpong	4,760
31	Pashoke	17 (26 from Pedang)	11 „ Rangaroon	3,300
32	Teesta Bridge	19 (*Viâ* Rungit)	3½	710
		22 (*Viâ* Pashoke)		
33	Riang	25 or 27	6	625
34	Kalijhora	32 (*Viâ* Teesta Bridge)	7	550

Under the Ex. Engr., P. W. D.

4. The bungalows are available only to persons provided with passes. A separate pass must be obtained for each occupant or party for each bungalow whether going or returning.

I. *Fees.*—Eight annas for each person for occupation during the day up to a maximum charge of *eight rupees.* One rupee per night for each occupant.

　1. In the case of Senchal, Rangaroon, and Badamtam the charge for occupation by day only is four annas for each person up to a maximum of four rupees.
　2. Passes may be cancelled by the local authorities without payment of compensation.
　3. A refund of bungalow fees is not allowed after the issue of a pass.
　4. Passes must be made over to the chowkidar in charge.
　5. Fees are payable in advance to the Deputy Commissioner or Executive Engineer on the submission of the application for the pass.
　6. Government officers on duty are allowed to occupy the bungalows free of charge.

II. *Furniture, etc.*—1. Beds, tables, chairs, lamps with wicks, candlesticks, crockery, glass and kitchen utensils are provided at each bungalow.
　2. Visitors must take their own bedding, cutlery, linen, candles, oil for lamps, and provisions.

III. *Provisions, etc.*—1. Ordinary bazar supplies are obtainable at Jorepokri, Dentam, Kalimpong, Teesta Bridge, Pedong, Namchi, Pakyong, and Ari.
　2. Firewood is provided free of charge on the Nepal frontier road bungalows. At Kalimpong four annas a maund is payable.

IV. *Accommodation.*—1. There is accommodation for six persons at bungalows 1 to 3, 5 to 15, 26 and 27. Nos. 16, 19, 20, 21, 22, 24, 25, and 28 have three rooms.
　2. Bungalows 17 and 18 to 23 have only two rooms.
　3. Two persons can be accommodated at the remaining bungalows, unless visitors take their own camp beds. At No. 29 the upper part of a monastery is used.

Wooden huts only, with two small rooms in each, and no furniture, but suitable for men wishing to fish. "Singlip" is called "Ligsip" on the map.

V. Servants.—1. A sweeper can be hired on the spot at Kalimpong, Jorepokri, Teesta Bridge, Rhenock, Ari, and Gantok.

    2. Elsewhere travellers must take sweepers with them, and no pass will issue, except on this condition.

    3. There is no resident khansamah at any bungalow.

VI. Situation.—1.

On the Nepal frontier road . . . Nos.	7 to 10
In Sikkim . . . . „	11 to 29
On the road to the Jelap Pass . . . „	18 to 20
On the Teesta valley road . . . . „	32 to 34
On the road to the Lachen valley . . . „	26 to 29

Namchi and Song are on the Darjeeling-Gantok road (*viâ* Rungeet Bazar).

Pakyong is on the Pedong-Gantok road.

Rissisum is on the Daling road to the plains.

VII. Tours.—The following tours can be made:—

    (*a*) Darjeeling to Jorepokri, Tonglu, Sandakphu, Phalut, Chiabhanjan, Dentam, Pamiongchi, Rinchimpong, Chakong and back to Darjeeling.

    (*b*) Darjeeling to Badamtam, Teesta Bridge, Pashoke and back to Darjeeling.

    (*c*) Darjeeling to Badamtam or Pashoke, Teesta Bridge, Riang, Kalijhora, Siliguri and back by train to Darjeeling.

    (*d*) Darjeeling, Badamtam or Pashoke, Kalimpong, Rissisum, Pedong, Ari, Sedonchen to Gnatong (for the Jelap pass) and back.

    (*e*) Darjeeling to Pedong, Pakyong, Gantok, Song, Namchi and back to Darjeeling.

    (*f*) Darjeeling to Gantok, Tumlong, Samatek, Toong and Cheongtong (for Lachen Lachung).

VIII. Rates.—For coolie rates see the prescribed table of rates separately.

    Eight annas a day is an average charge for each coolie hired in Darjeeling, four annas if hired in Kalimpong, and six annas in Sikkim.

IX. Map.—A map of the locality can be obtained at the Office of the Deputy Commissioner. Price one rupee.

RICHD. T. GREER,

Deputy Commissioner,

Darjeeling.

6th August 1897.

N.B.—The original spelling which has been adopted by the Deputy Commissioner of Darjeeling and which differs slightly from that in the Route Book has been adhered to in this notice.